HOW TO BE AN ARTIST

This is a book about how to develop your creativity.

If you want to tap into that unexplored part of yourself that gets bulldozed by work, commitments or lack of space, then this is the book for you.

I believe that you can grow your artist in a nurturing and supportive way, giving it the time and resources to develop and blossom.

This is a book that takes the inner artist seriously – the playful, the complicated, the difficult part – leading it on a journey that includes starting, building a practice and planning long term goals.

If you are an experienced practitioner, there is also much to discover in this book about getting in touch again with the key ideals that drew you to creativity in the first place.

For everyone, I suggest reading the book from page one onwards, or alternatively dipping into it, using your artist's compass to recognise that wherever you begin, and on whatever page, wherever you find yourself, is exactly the right place for you.

HOW
TO BE AN
ARTIST

MICHAEL ATAVAR

Kiosk
PUBLISHING

info@how-to-be-an-artist.com
www.how-to-be-an-artist.com

Copyright © 2009 Michael Atavar
First published in 2009 by Kiosk Publishing
Third edition 2014

ISBN 978-0-9531073-1-5
A catalogue record for this book is available
from the British Library.

Designed by Rose-Innes Associates
Typeset in Trade Gothic

Semper incipimus

Who is an artist? The answer is you.

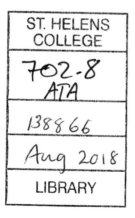

CONTENTS

HOW TO START

What You Will Learn In This Section

- How to start.
- How to deal with the blank page.
- Simple methods for beginning.

I believe that in order to start you need to be positive with regard to your own creativity.

Understand that all creative activity is about the practice of starting. Each day presents a new blank page. Learning appropriate structures can help allay the fear that we all have of a new enterprise.

Part One offers simple techniques, top tips and useful activities to help you begin.

Take your time.

BLANK PAPER

The piece of paper is in front of you. You might feel afraid. But courage, my friend.

Pick up a pen and without thinking begin to write. It's not important what it is, or what you say, simply write.

Within this automatism, these endless words, you will begin to see sentences and structures form. Perhaps they don't mean anything yet, but that's OK. You have got over the first hurdle – the emptiness of the white page.

That's the good news. The bad news is that you will always meet this feeling. It's part of being an artist, being creative. Your choice, your journey is to address this sense, each time you start. With practice, and with endless attempts, it will get easier.

The page starts to look inviting, open, challenging, even warm. It holds enrapture, magic, possibility.

The energy that you feel when beginning to write will carry you forward, beyond the first page, into all your writing.

Follow the energy, follow the road, follow the words – let the sentences take you with them.

Pick up a pen and without thinking begin to write. It's not important what it is, or what you say, simply write.

HOW TO START

The only thing that I can tell you about how to start is that –

THE ONLY WAY TO START IS TO START.

What I mean by this is that you can't start in the abstract, in your head. I've never seen that done. The only way to start is to start now. To write on a page, to draw, paint, dance, perform – whatever form it takes.

And when it does start, it immediately changes. That change creates energy and the energy is what enables the work.

If you only stay in the abstract this never happens.

All those plans, fantasies, dreams, intentions of making something, being an artist, never change through doing. They aren't challenged through realisation. They don't have to meet with reality. And so they remain inert, removed, absent.

Only in the making can things happen. It doesn't really matter that much what the making is. It just matters that you make something.

Making is a process. It changes, grows, adapts, turns back, loses the plot, returns.

The beginning may eventually become the end or be abandoned or come back in three months, but this time different.

Often I find that the first paragraph, or first sentence, or page you write will contain the whole work in capsule form. The task is then to expand it, stretch it, work with it over a long period to become the piece. The same is true for an image, a movement, a sound.

Remember, one line can become the work.

Notice that the fear of beginning is bigger than the actuality of doing.

I recently met a colleague who was thinking of starting a course, which was a difficult endeavour. She said to me, 'But before I start my training I need to finish my flat. Then I feel I can completely concentrate on the task. I'll get someone to sand the floors and I really need to sort out some storage, so all my papers are close at hand.'

I said, quoting something I remembered from Kodo Sawaki, a Zen Monk, 'Be careful. Start today! You can't put off this until tomorrow. Your self-development is at stake. Begin doing something now.'

Instead of finishing off the flat then moving to her course, I think perhaps her course would have helped her accept her flat as it was.

Oh also –

THE ONLY WAY TO MAKE THE WORK IS TO MAKE
THE WORK.

There is no substitute for making the work. You can
organise, delegate, fundraise, negotiate, develop all
you like but the work only gets made in the rehearsal
room or the studio. This place for rehearsal can even
be your front room, or your bedroom – don't let a lack
of space derail you.

(I expect you were thinking that.)

Remember, you are devious. You will try anything
to avoid the work. All your excuses are delusion. All
your worries about money/space/resources are a way
of taking energy from the work and putting it into
other areas.

Be mindful of your own ability to fool yourself.

I've lost count of the number of artists who say they
can't make the work until a grant/resource/bursary
comes through. Although I understand the difficulties
faced by artists stuck in their own homes – the reality
is not that they can't make the work, but that it feels
too difficult.

If so, create a big piece, but make it your long-term
ambition.

In the meantime generate some smaller experiments on your own. Who knows these short, immediate ideas might come together eventually to create your masterwork.

Twenty Things To Do To Start

- Write something on paper.
- Draw a line, draw a shape.
- Turn inward and think of an image, then write about it.
- Describe the contents of the room you are in now.
- Describe the view.
- Describe anything in minute detail.
- Write everything that happens in your day, every day.
- Pay attention to your dreams, write them up, use them as plot lines.
- Think of your life as fiction or a movie.
- Put ideas in a hat and commit to doing whatever gets picked out.
- Work on your train journey to work. Ten minutes each day.
- Work in your lunch hour. Write or draw on the napkin of the café where you regularly eat.
- If you can't write a novel, then write poetry.
- Space to work is not necessary, create space in your head.
- Abandon any project over five years old and begin again.
- Don't rely on other people to start for you.

- Stop watching TV, thereby decreasing by 50% your possibility of distraction.
- Don't read back, or look at what you have made.
- Don't ask other people's opinion.
- Don't ask other people's permission.

Notice that the fear of beginning is bigger than the actuality of doing.

PEN, NOTEPAD, EYE

Wherever I go, I carry a pen and notepad around with me.

It's always a ring-bound shorthand pad, of about eighty sheets. You will have your preference, just go with your own instinct.

This is your main instrument of inspiration, so cherish it, buy what you need, love it, care for it – and never let it out of your sight. Wherever you are and wherever you go, make sure you have access to paper and a pen.

If possible don't write on scraps of napkin or cigarette packets. It's OK but not as good. Look after your work, cherish it from the beginning, archive it well. Over the course of years I've come to fetishise certain types of basic stationery, believing that the magic resides in their dull, blank surfaces. It's not true, it's in me, but this lie about materials is useful, as otherwise I would find it hard to start.

It feels that there is something beautiful, mysterious in the blank white page, the empty stage.

Take your notepad with you everywhere that you go and don't be ashamed to write in it. Use it on the bus, in the kitchen, on a train, at the airport, on your sofa, in bed.

You must get over the self-consciousness of being seen. You are an artist, remember, that's who you are now.

Everyone's going to know sooner or later...

I write everywhere I go. Not in complete narratives, often not even in sentences. Just scraps, ideas, fragments, names. It doesn't matter, sort it out later. The main thing is to write what you see. Use your eyes. Anything that you see is interesting, so note it down.

Making concrete is important.

As long as these ideas, descriptions stay in your head, they will not become realised. You need to coax them down, make them real. The concretisation is an important part of the process – it makes it actual.

Make contact with yourself through the channel of the pen on the paper. There is something elemental here, benign, furious, ignited. Be in touch with that feeling whether it be calm, beautiful, elegiac or pounding, angry, flooded.

You are the source, discover yourself.

Twenty Ways To Use A Notepad

- Write in it.
- Draw in it.
- Write down quotes in it.
- Write down overheard conversations in it.
- Write down your dreams in it as if they were a script.
- Write a page of first lines in it.
- Write a page of titles in it.
- Write a page of characters' names in it.
- Write a page of imaginary cities in it.
- Write in it with fire, water, earth, air.
- Let the rain fall on it, dulling the ink and collate what you can still read.
- Balance the notepad on your head whilst you think for ten minutes about what you will write, directing the energy towards the paper.
- Put the notepad on the floor and use as a step for you to walk on, moving you up.
- Lie on the floor and put your notepad on your stomach, breathing inspiration into it.
- Put the notepad over your heart and pay attention to what it says.
- Flip rapidly through your written pages, piecing a sentence together from all the random bits.
- Read each page as a series of titles, or a series of titles as a text.
- Write down whatever comes when you address the blank page.

- Write down whatever comes, don't think.
- Write down whatever comes, like breathing.

Take your notepad with you everywhere that you go and don't be ashamed to write in it.

SORT IT OUT LATER

You are an information gatherer, you are an eye. Everything you see is interesting. Learn to believe in this and fashion your world towards the recording of that data.

So –

- Pen
- Paper
- Brush
- Camera
- Ink

are all vital ingredients to you.

Don't be critical of what you see. It's your world, your vision. You brought it into being when you were born and you will take it away again. Everything is you, so record it, look after it.

The voices of criticism – parents, colleagues, even friends who can be quick to dissect you – are especially difficult when you are starting out with a new practice. Don't internalise this by becoming your biggest critic.

Start by simply recording and sort it out later.

Record –

- The place you live.
- Your room.
- Your friends.
- Your view.
- The journey to work.
- The night sky.
- The train on the way home.
- The pavement litter.
- Neon signs.
- The trees.
- The birds you see.
- Leaves.

Everything is your process and worthy of attention, so don't let anything skip your grasp. All is art and can be fuel for your artistic endeavours.

The more you go into this recording mode, the more you will see. So detail becomes important. The glistening lino on the floor of the underground carriage, the colour of the sky at particular times of day, the debris and litter on the streets of your town. All is available and miraculously all is free. Take advantage.

Whilst in this recording mode, don't worry about what you will make, what final product.

Just take the temperature.

You can sort it out later, put it into order. This is not an abnegation of responsibility, it's just freeing up space for yourself to play, to dream, to magnetise.

Play is the most important thing. See these images, these ideas as Lego bricks. You build them up, you knock them down, you play around, you invent.

Your work is like a spaceship tethered to Earth, it can take you for a ride around the universe. Be bold, go, but remember to write down all the details.

Twenty Ways To Sort It Out Later

- Sort it out according to colour of material.
- Sort it out according to key words.
- Sort it out according to sense of place, geography.
- Sort it out according to smell, taste, touch.
- Sort it out backwards.
- Sort it out very S-L-O-W-L-Y.
- Sort it out in random fashion.
- Sort it out but leave most things out.
- Sort it out according to magic principles.
- Sort it out as you would a recipe.
- Sort it out languidly.
- Sort it out as at a shooting range, fast and furious.
- Sort it out over time.
- Sort it out accidentally.
- Sort it out dangerously.

- Sort it out but leave everything in.
- Sort it out boldly.
- Sort it out like you are about to die.
- Sort it out like you have discovered you will actually live.
- Sort it out yourself.

Record the
place you live,
your room,
your friends,
your view.

BE SEEN

One of the most difficult ways of starting is stepping into the role of artist. Or even using the 'A' word. Don't worry, it took me years to accept that what I was doing was really art.

However, it is useful, in your dialogues with other people, to be clear about what you do, your status, your view of it and where your practice is going.
In fact this understanding is part of the process of becoming an artist.

After all, if you don't take the work or yourself seriously, no one ever will.

- Step into the spotlight.
- Be unapologetic about what you do.
- Take up space.
- Allow the world to see you.

Being seen is a difficulty faced by most artists I work with. Even the most upfront practitioners have some problems stepping into their own power and meeting the world head on.

Deep down surely all art is about needing to be seen?

Step into the space.

Here Are A Few Tips For Being Visible

- Have a business card/CV/website to hand.
- Meet people boldly and energetically. Try to be as clear as possible.
- Don't use 'should', 'perhaps' or 'possibly' in your statement. Be definite, definitive.
- Don't say what you can't do, say what you can do and your strategies for future development.
- Take up space, form a company, even in name only.
- Love your mistakes, they are what make you great.
- Don't be anyone's assistant.
- Don't wait for power to be conferred on you or you will wait forever, grab it now.
- Generate your own projects, or constellate a group of other artists to show, make or exhibit together.
- Act as though you are a character in a film, a fantasy figure and when you call up, or post your CV/script/DVD, behave with the confidence of that character. It's not really you that applies for the grant/job/fund and so not you that has to deal with the success or failure of your grant/job/fund. It's your character's ups and downs that you will observe.

Your CV is a canvas for the ever-changing vista of your practice. Update it regularly, moulding it to suit the new landscape in which you find yourself.

Top Tip

If you send a CV out with your application make
sure that you do the work for the reader. Most
people have busy working lives and are unlikely to
read everything you send or extrapolate information
from your statement. You need to highlight any
narratives/themes/motifs for them and package
this information clearly and credibly.

Under no circumstances expect anyone to do the
work for you.

It just won't happen.

Your CV is a canvas for the ever-changing vista of your practice.

SIMPLICITY

The best delivery is simplicity.

Just deliver one good idea well.

What's your idea? Define it in one paragraph, one sentence, one word.

Some suggestions –

- Chaos.
- Autobiography.
- Renewal.
- Complexity.
- Melancholy.
- Absence.
- Realism.

What's your word?

Others are –

- Amplification.
- Reversal.
- Duplication.
- Singularity.
- Mass.
- Superimposition.

- By 'amplification' I mean turning up the volume on any one element, until it grows prominent, or distorts.
- By 'reversal' I mean doing something the opposite of what's expected, or putting two contradictory things together.
- By 'duplication' I mean making a series with a complex of relationships or meanings.
- By 'singularity' I mean working with one element to the exclusion of all others.
- By 'mass' I mean adding or taking away volume to overwhelm or entice the viewer.
- By 'superimposition' I mean layering one or more things on top of each other, sometimes the same, sometimes different, often adding a dream-like quality in the process.

If you work with these key concepts you can't go far wrong.

Simplicity is one of the most basic building blocks of artwork.

Beware that an over reliance on art theory can pull you into a space where you stop working with the simple qualities of your own materials.

Irony can stop you breathing.

But back to simplicity...

Here is a recipe for an egg sandwich I got in Taiwan.
I ate this dish from a street stall in the market.
It's probably my favourite, simplest meal.

I include it here as an odd adjunct to the main text,
to throw something unexpected into the mix.

Taiwan Fried Egg Sandwich
Chop some spring onions. Toast two slices of white
bread, so that they very slightly start to brown. No
butter. Fry a fresh organic egg on both sides in a frying
pan until it's cooked but still runny. Sprinkle spring
onions on one slice of bread, squirt on some chilli
sauce to taste, add the egg, then the other slice.
Eat hot.

Top Tip
Complexity can be achieved through the accumulation
of several simple ideas running in parallel to each other.

Add and just keep adding. Subtract and just keep
taking away.

Work with what you have and can see around you
every day. For example, if the room you are working
in only has three chairs, a light and a microphone,
then that becomes the content of the work.

Turn up and turn down the volume on the mic, until it becomes overwhelming, unbearable.

Bring your difficulty about making the work into the work itself.

Lastly, remember, don't exclude anything. Make everything you see and feel part of the process.

Just deliver one good idea well.

AMPLIFICATION

Cultivate a language, a vocabulary that's integral to you, to your practice, to your audience. Turn the pointer to you and work out who you are.

But how do you do this, especially at the beginning of your career when your work is likely to be derivative and generic? How can you avoid sounding and looking like someone else? Answer – be an amplifier for one idea, no more than one simple thing. Find out what it is, do an exhaustive inventory and then amplify it 200 times, 1,000 times, 1 million times. I'm not joking.

Amplification is the basic building block of all art, all creative activity. Find one simple idea and build on it – fast, slow, inverted, forward, splintered, whole.

So, for example, if there are five in the company and that's the basic, fundamental material of your practice, focus on the stories that the five of you make, how your lives intertwine, your co-operation, your physical needs, your household waste, anything. It all comes down to five. Similarly if you work in site-specific spaces, don't just say that (there are many companies doing this nowadays), focus on the qualities of the spaces, their nature, the temporal conditions, the collaboration, the uniqueness of the walls, the halls, the doorways, the rooms.

As an afterthought – another psychoanalytic technique, word association, that works very well to unlock blocks.

Try it this way –

Exercise To Unlock Blocks

You will need two people.

Choose a quiet room with no distractions.

Sit opposite each other. The 'interviewer' (A) just sits and notices. The 'one who has blocks' (B) speaks.

A invites B to speak, to list at random a number of items, anything that comes into their head. They start to speak and at some point B will stop. A asks B what is in their mind. What's the image, the word that was on the tip of the tongue when the break occurred? This is the idea that needs work on. It's the concept around which there is a blockage.

Discuss. Swap partners and repeat.

In a world of increasing complexity, it might appear as though these basic building blocks of simplicity and amplification are naïve or rudimentary.

Try them and see.

Most art relies on these qualities. As a beginner it's worth sticking to these basic principles to see what happens.

Select one technique and try it out today. Or look for modern artists that use these processes.

Pursue a methodology as if it were a river, moving in one direction.

Where do you get to?

Amplification

is the basic building block of all art. Find one simple idea and build on it – fast, slow, inverted, forward, splintered, whole.

MOOD BOARD

Another way of starting is to make collections, or accumulations of things, putting them together in order to notice what you find attractive or interesting. Sometimes these arrangements of objects can become the work itself, at other times they provide a useful artist's compass, pointing you in the right direction.

I'm looking at some pictures and photographs as they appeared on a wall in photographer Diane Arbus's 70s apartment. There are photos, newspaper clippings, postcards, found images, Polaroids – sellotaped together or pinned to the wall in a large collage.

This is an excellent example of a mood board.

A mood board is a collection of found images, ideas that currently inspire you. It's like a signature. Throughout your creative career this signature will change. You'll pick up different ideas, different influences.

A mood board will alert you to these changes.

'Everything I picked up this month is blue' or 'Weirdly all of a sudden I seem to be interested in faces'.

So a mood board is not just a collection, it's a springboard into something new.

A mood board could be –

- A collection of newspaper clippings.
- A collection of postcards from galleries or museums.
- A collection of labels from your local supermarket.
- A collection of colour swatches.
- A collection of objects.
- A collection of songs on a CD.
- A collection of things that are found on the street.

Some of my favourite things to collect are the paint swatches you get for free in DIY shops. Large carousels of colour. Choose a few to take with you, to set the tone for this month.

Other free things are –

- Museum/gallery brochures advertising art shows (most of these can be found in coffee shops or restaurants).
- Carpet samples.
- Free newspapers.
- Flyers through the door for pizza and fast food restaurants.

Look at everything with your 'art glasses' on.

Art is often created through the re-imagining of ordinary things. Remember Andy Warhol's silkscreens of beauty ads? Don't discard anything as too cheap, not elevated enough, not sanctified as 'art'.

Mood boards can put you in touch with the magic of everyday things and enlarge your practice through the acceptance of the idea that everything and anything can be art.

Art is everything that you see. Look through your eyes at the world and make a statement about what you observe.

Art is often created through the re-imagining of ordinary things.

IT DOESN'T HAVE TO BE PERFECT NOW

I don't believe in perfection.

I don't believe it's achievable or interesting. I don't believe I should spend my time doing one perfect thing.

A big block to our creativity is the fear that our work, even in its initial stages, has to meet the standards of other completed artworks – published novels, gallery shows, staged plays. This is not how work is actually made. It doesn't arrive completed or ready packaged like a microwaved meal. These plays and novels went through many revisions, with a series of mentors, editors, dramaturges.

This fantasy of perfection that we conjure up is often used to disempower ourselves, creating a standard of completed perfection that we can't ever meet, so making it easy and convenient for us never to begin.

So one part of your process of starting is allowing yourself to be yourself, whether successful or naïve, beginner or loser (it could in fact be all these things). It doesn't matter. You can only be where you are now.

Have ambition, yet try to avoid creating a fantasy of the future – publication, output, exhibition – in order to empower your inner critic and so silence your own true voice.

These days I see creativity as a process. Along the way, in time, during this sequence, you might make some things which could be called artworks. However, rather than being the clear focus of the work, these objects are the residues of a complex process that has happened to you.

Other people, who are not the artist, might look at these as completed works, but you could more helpfully look at these things as old photo albums, interesting, but not necessarily where you are now. Part of you, but not the whole story.

If you get an exhibition, that's great, otherwise you just keep on working, as you always have done.

In this version of art, preparation becomes perfection. Your goal is the day-to-day running of your artistic life, nothing more and nothing less. Prepare the ground, have ideas, work with what is and you will always be OK.

Top Tip
Be generous to yourself.

Treat your work as if it were a plant on your window sill. Nurture it. Have a relationship with it. Talk to it. Eventually, after several weeks, it will reward you with a flower.

Twenty Things To Do To Stop Being Perfect

- Allow fragments.
- Encourage the temporary, the coming and going of your practice.
- Create a good flow of energy – completion and throwing away being key daily elements.
- Write 100 scenes rather than a big narrative.
- Don't create unreachable aims, for example comparing your painting with one hanging in a major gallery.
- Instead think about an important work of art made in your front room. Strip art of its context.
- Celebrate failure and success every day.
- Think of art as a process.
- Think of art as recycling.
- Think of the imagination as a process.
- Scraps are like compost, keep noting them, until they create a flower bed.
- Creativity is not located in objects.
- Creativity is not located in other people.
- Creativity is not located in reviews.
- Who cares what other people think, do, make, respond etc. – it's you we're dealing with here.
- Don't archive other people's work.
- Put contradictory things together.
- Put matching things together.
- Put pointless things together.
- Put stupid things together.

Be generous to yourself. Treat your work as if it were a plant. Talk to it. Eventually, after several weeks, it will reward you with a flower.

ABBA

Often what you need to know is right under your nose.

An artist came to see me about forming a performance company.

When I asked her, 'What's the name?' she appeared stuck. I suggested that she use the old ABBA routine of taking some of the letters from the participants' names to form a new word. It could be 'nonsense', it didn't matter.

This idea fitted in with the concept of her play.

She happened to mention that the team was a very disparate group, with ages ranging from twenty-two to fifty-seven. I didn't see that as a drawback. In fact I saw it as a selling point. '22257' i.e. twenty-two to fifty-seven seemed like a good company name to me.

Similarly put scraps in a hat and pull them out one at a time –

- Old newspapers.
- Pieces of dialogue.
- Written narratives.
- Sweet wrappers.

So –

- Let chance give you something.
- Let chance decide the form of the piece or at least inform your own process, whilst you're still making the work.
- Let chance be your friend.

Don't concretise. Let play still happen. Remain fluid, mobile, ready to throw things away, even up to the last minute.

Don't work so hard – let it all come to you easily.

- Look under your nose.
- All the material you will ever need is always within your grasp.
- Smell, touch, taste.
- What's in front of you?
- How does it feel – intimately.
- Struggle to describe it to me.
- Play with it.

What have you forgotten?

Let play still happen. Remain fluid, mobile, ready to throw things away, even up to the last minute.

DOTTED LINE TECHNIQUE

I work with a technique called the dotted line.

- - - -

For me the dotted line simply and elegantly represents the journey of the artist, taking small steps, always in one long line, moving out into the future.

Just do one thing today. It doesn't really matter what it is. Just do it.

The only thing that I insist on is that the thing you do can't be administration, organising, application writing, phone calls. It has to be one creative thing.

Your challenge is –

- To begin.
- To make something every day.
- To not stop to look back until you've finished.
- Then edit.
- Then end.

So the process would be about not letting the critical voice inside your head inhibit you. That voice may be the voice of a parent, a friend, a colleague, a fellow artist.

The voice says –

- 'Why are you doing that?'
- 'It's going to be shit, so why not stop now, save yourself all that heartache?'
- 'You'll never be an artist.'
- 'You've left it until you're too old/you're not qualified/you've got no talent.'
- 'X artist (substitute your current obsession) is the one they really like. They'll get the grant/job/residency.'
- 'I'll never get an exhibition/publishing deal/contract anyway.'

A critical voice that polices out creativity.

'What IS it anyway?' (I read some of these comments in a book I found in a charity shop. Someone had written a list of the hateful things people had said about their art and then forgotten to take the sheet of paper out of it when they got rid of the book. Some of these phrases hit me very directly. The 'What IS it anyway?' was especially wounding. Even to this day people say this about my work.)

But...

As artists we can survive this critical voice. In fact it might be a part of us that we have to engage with, have to listen to, in order to become stronger.

In order to get by, I use the dotted line technique, taking each step in that line as an individual victory. No Turner Prize ambitions for me, just small celebrations of continuous achievement.

In the dotted line technique, we say –

- 'It's one step.'
- 'All steps are equal.'
- 'Steps are what we do every day. Like walking to the bank. Like walking to work.'
- 'Steps just keep coming, one by one.'
- 'Each one is measured, cool. Each one is a journey.'
- 'Steps build something. They go somewhere.'

Steps are the positive choices that we can make, the ones that rarely come out when the bullying parental voice is around, filling the space. But these steps have equal value to the loud, negative shouting of that overbearing voice. Sometimes, if we practise, they can even cancel it out.

What I especially like about the dotted line technique and its individual steps is that –

- It's positive.
- It looks to the future.
- It's practical – it makes things happen.
- It provides structure.

Top Tip

Build a calendar for your wall. Like the scratches
on a prison cell.

I
II
III
IV
V
VI
VII
VIII
IX
X

Every day put a tick when your creative steps are
completed. Keep going until the chart is full.

Just do one thing today. It doesn't really matter what it is.

Just do it.

ONE SENTENCE

Use one single sentence to describe yourself. Use this sentence to identify what makes you different from other artists.

Take care of this sentence – it's the most important thing you own. It has monetary value.

In writing this sentence, range far and wide, but don't also forget what's under your nose. For example, it often strikes me that artists fail to mention their cultural background, or sexuality, when it's relevant to their work. Even if it's not directly related, it informs how you got there, and helps someone make a decision about your work.

Make any statement, letter, application come from you. You are the source.

A common problem is that artists, keen to disguise their very creativity, and desperate to adopt a business model, make far too formal approaches to galleries/funders/promoters. The language becomes very abbreviated, narrow. Instead think creatively. Approach them in the manner or style of your work.

Put yourself in their shoes. Imagine how many CVs they get every week. How many packs of slides, how many scripts looking for feedback.

- Be creative.
- Be adventurous.
- Be bold.
- Be daring.
- Take risks.
- Add images.
- Add propositions.
- Give them a pitch.
- If you're a playwright, send your pitch in using blank verse.
- If you're a painter, use watercolours or oils.
- If you're a performance artist, put on a free live art show outside their office.

I rarely go to see artists' work. The ones I tend to respond to, send me more than an invite, or even a personal letter. The ones I go and see somehow trigger my imagination, reach in through my window and touch me personally.

Top Tip
Artists are afraid of offending funders – saying the wrong thing. They tend to make statements about their practice that are very conservative, all-embracing, bland, generic – as if they want to cover all bases, all eventualities. In fact this is completely the wrong strategy.

What makes you different, unique is the very thing you need to accent.

Find your bit of grit.

Is it –

- That you bring opera to clubs?
- That you work with OAPs on holiday coaches?
- That you perform on rooftops?
- That you make improvised street games?

Clearly I've exaggerated here for the benefit of effect.

Do you get the idea?

Twenty Things To Put In Your Sentence

- Something about you.
- Something personal.
- Something about your age.
- Something about your background.
- Something about your race.
- Something unusual.
- Something contradictory.
- Something delicate.
- Something professional.
- Something bold.
- Something dangerous.
- Something about your history.
- Something about the future.
- Something about your relationship to form.
- Something about your relationship to others.
- Something about your relationship to audience.
- Something about your relationship to collision or harmony.
- Something unpredictable.
- Something not faked.
- Something real.

Make any statement, letter, application come from you. You are the source.

ONE LONG LINE

In a world that's speeding up, one of the responsibilities of the artist might be to slow things down. To S-T-R-E-T-C-H things out in one long time-line.

One of the simplest and most effective techniques is to slow something down.

- Make it long.
- Make it longer.
- Make it even longer still.

It's a wonderful means of generating new material.

Just the other day I was listening to the track 'Spule', from Kraftwerk 2 (1971) – the sound of breathing slowed down, with some splintered guitar arpeggios over the top.

It sounded completely fresh and alive, not at all over thirty years old.

S-T-R-E-T-C-H it out –

- Until breaking point.
- Until endurance becomes unbearable.
- Until every little detail becomes visible.

I personally want a performance that is –

- 24 hours.
- 7 days.
- 7 years.
- A lifetime long.

Like the work of American artist Linda Montano.

(I once saw LM give a performance at the ICA, London, where each audience member was given a free avocado and everyone was encouraged to go up on to the stage, during the performance, to get a head and shoulder massage.)

If the work that you are making gets stuck, slow it down. Slow yourself down and see what happens. Perhaps something will come, perhaps it will reveal a new approach.

I'd like to make a work that takes Kraftwerk's theme and create a piece that is just one breath.

'One Breath' (2009).

Instructions – make a work that is just one breath.

Experiment with how this can be done. How can you capture one breath, make the moment last one lifetime?

Top Tip

An idea can be transformed by its relationship to time.

One of the simplest and most effective techniques is to slow something down.

WORKING WITH LIMITATIONS

It might appear that what I am offering you is
something that can't yet be achieved. It feels too
distant, too far off, too big – something that's not
connected to where you are now. Perhaps it feels
too early in your career to address the wider issues
of the art world?

However you are in the perfect place to work in a
highly imaginative way. You have nothing and so
can create successfully from a unique standpoint.

Your limits are your benefits.

Perhaps you don't fully understand what painting is –
great, then bring something original to that form.
Similarly someone told you that you are a performance
artist – great, you don't quite understand what that is,
but you can still make something on a stage that is
uniquely your own.

Limits are the necessary structures that support us,
hold us in, give us hope.

So –

- If you don't have a studio, use your kitchen table.
- If you don't have canvas, use newsprint.
- If you can't afford oils, use house paint.

- If you can't afford to make theatre, perform monologues.
- If you have no concept of selling, create ideas art.
- If you're not intellectual, make work that explores naïvety.
- If you can't sculpt with marble, use polystyrene.
- If you can't write a novel, pen haikus.

At all times, use what you can't do to your advantage, making something unique out of an absence of the correct thing. So, for example, if you can't afford stone, wood or marble, investigate the properties of cardboard, polystyrene and papier-mâché. Then the work becomes a unique relationship to the material and its salvage, its qualities affording an imaginative, exciting presence in the world.

Always investigate what's closest to home, right under your nose. Don't set your sights on impossible tasks, with the immanent possibility of failure. Take advantage of what falls into your lap, breathing its sweetness.

So –

- If you can't find a publisher, write a blog, or print up some pamphlets and sell them to bookshops.
- If you can't interest a gallery, book an empty shop for a month and put on a group show.

- If a major institution won't mount your play, do guerrilla-style street performances outside the National Theatre.
- If your concept art isn't getting any attention, draw with chalk or water on the pavements, every day a new slogan.

Also, remember that if your practice is a failure, make a fly-on-the-wall documentary about the process of rejection, feeding it back into your artwork.

Art is every day. It isn't solely the province of glossy monthly magazines with shows in Berlin, New York and São Paulo.

Art is local to you, where you are now, in all its gritty dichotomy.

Art is local
to you, where
you are now,
in all its gritty
dichotomy.

VOICES OF CRITICISM

To end this section of the book, it might be useful to mention again the voices of criticism that sometimes stifle your creativity and stop you from even beginning in the first place.

'It won't be any good', 'It'll never get published', 'X artist is so much better', 'They know people in the art world,' 'I can't call myself a professional artist', 'It's just a hobby for me'.

Do any of these phrases seem familiar?

Sometimes you might be able to name these voices. They might remind you of a parent, a former teacher, a fellow artist, a negative friend. However, often these voices, these criticisms are so buried inside you that it appears as if it's you speaking.

UNDERSTAND THAT THESE VOICES OF CRITICISM ARE NOT REALLY YOU.

It's an illusion. It might appear like that, but it comes from somewhere else, a long way off, and now doesn't apply to you. You have already been there, it is something you once did, it's the past, now you can let it go, it's time to move forward.

You are free.

We are all beginners.

In my world of art practice, we cultivate this feeling every day. It's OK to begin. Every time you meet the empty page, the canvas, the open stage, you are a beginner. Anyone who believes that they have a pre-ordained right not to be a beginner is seriously deluded.

Beginning is every day. Beginning is life.

So to end this section I offer –

Twenty Ways To Work With Voices Of Criticism

- Don't ask permission from anyone. It's a car crash path to disaster.
- Don't wait for a grant/bursary/award to confirm your status.
- Only ask for feedback if you really believe that you need it and only from trusted friends and colleagues.
- Don't mass mail scripts/novels/ideas.
- Don't cold call.
- Find a supportive context for your work, build relationships.
- Create your own network.
- Don't project your identity into some mythical, faraway future.
- Don't keep working on any idea over five years old.

- Don't ask for feedback from a partner, a friend, or a parent who doesn't understand the genre in which you are working. It's likely to be a demoralising experience.
- Be a critic, a journalist for your own work.
- Don't offer support to other practitioners, in the hope that you will receive a sympathetic ear in return.
- Don't overinflate your own ego. You will crash.
- Don't hide away, your ego will shrink to fit the confines of your room.
- Start a magazine to promote your work and material of a similar nature.
- Never let a parent dictate your options.
- Take all criticism with a healthy pinch of disdain. It usually has an agenda.
- Listen carefully to feedback. You might actually learn something, or even better, be given a good idea for free.
- Keep going.
- Keep making work.

Listen carefully
to feedback. You might actually learn something, or even better, be given a good idea for free.

2

DEVELOPING A PRACTICE

What You Will Learn In This Section

- How to grow your artist's practice.
- How to build a vocabulary for your work.
- Using your intuition and curiosity to create a language that's distinctively your own.

I believe that growth and nurture are key elements in your journey.

If you don't practise your creativity, it won't flourish. Being an artist, or developing your creativity, is a daily activity. I suggest strategic elements to introduce these features into your life.

Part Two offers complementary strategies that address difficulty, creating a strong artistic language.

The task is to build growth.

INVITATION TO PROCESS

So you've already started but what do you do next?

How do you continue to develop a practice within the demands of contemporary life? Perhaps you are working full-time, raising a family, making money or managing your employees. How do you fulfil your artist's practice within these tight constraints?

Even if you are lucky enough to be an artist all the time, how do you manage to develop a voice so it can be heard above the crowded landscape of the modern world?

The answer is to work systematically, using methods you learned in Part One like 'The Dotted Line Technique', making small steps, on a day-by-day basis, adding new strategies you will master in Part Two, working with blocks to unlock creative dead ends.

Abandon the idea of art as a series of necessary outputs. Rather think of your work as a process, allowing images and ideas to surface. Unlock your intuition. The solution to any creative puzzle is inside you, always present, available at any moment, if you are ready to look.

In this section process is your goal.

Process is all. It's the heartbeat of creativity.

Keep going.

You can do it.

Process is all.

It's the heartbeat of creativity.

NO MAGICAL MANAGER

There is no magical manager/agent/promoter that will make your life easier.

Someone that will take care of all the nasty business stuff so that you can just concentrate on performing/singing/painting/sculpting etc.

Sorry.

Probably the sooner you accept this the better. Then you can use all the energy you devoted to fantasy (have you worked out your Turner Prize acceptance speech yet?) and actually put it into your work here, today.

OK. So one out of a million may find the perfect business partner to support them but for most artists it's necessary to be –

- Artist
- Business manager
- Agent
- PR person
- Designer
- Fundraiser

all rolled into one.

Yes it's not ideal. But that's the reality.

And there wasn't a halcyon era in the 80s, 70s, 1900s or 17th century when artists were free just to create. There have always been patrons, kings, political structures etc. Think about it. Take off those blinkers.

I've lost count of the number of artists who've come to me looking for this one incredible person.

In fact the figure of the magical manager and the search for him/her is not only ultimately futile but dangerous to yourself. It defers power to someone else. Someone who can solve things. It's very disempowering for the individual.

Bring back the power to you now.

Focus on yourself here today and what you can do, in some small measure, to move yourself forward. Internalise this figure of the mythical magical manager.

Also think about the gender of this figure. Is it a man or woman? This will tell you about your own psychology. If you're keen to get a hustling, aggressive man, you would be advised to work on your own inner masculine. Alternatively if it's a holding, nurturing woman you crave, look to your own inner feminine. Note how present she is in your life. If she's not there much, try and coax her out.

So in terms of fantasy, the magical manager is the ultimate figure and should be avoided at all costs.

Remember an unfortunate truth – a manager or fundraiser will only work with you if you look like you're a good financial proposition. They want to make money.

If you still want a manager, shore up your money-making potential first.

A more accessible figure is that of the magician's assistant. This is a helper, colleague, collaborator, friend. Someone who will metaphorically help you pull rabbits out of hats.

The magician's assistant is an essential part of being an artist.

See if you can find someone who will –

- Build a website.
- Replace a bulb on a slide projector.
- Drive a van.
- Understand computers.
- Hand out your leaflets.
- Pour your water into a glass at your artist's talk.

These are acts of everyday magic – potentially more useful than a manager any day.

- Network.
- Collaborate.
- Develop friendships.
- Agitate.

Become a magician's assistant for someone else.

Offer to –

- Take their press photos.
- Make a badge.
- Throw a launch party.
- Drive their gear.

(Whatever's in your capacity.)

If you do, perhaps you can develop a relationship with another artist and you can mutually assist each other as magician's assistants.

That's real magic.

Focus on yourself here today and what you can do, in some small measure, to move yourself forward.

DEVELOPING A VOCABULARY

In my experience your artist's vocabulary comes out of you and your limitations. It's not something out there, beyond yourself, in a fantasy world, way off. It's close to home, under your nose, within reach, very obvious.

- Perhaps you like blue – that is your vocabulary.
- Perhaps your eyesight is poor – that is your vocabulary.
- Perhaps you only ever play minor chords – that is your vocabulary.
- Perhaps you work collaboratively – that is your vocabulary.
- Perhaps your mind goes off at tangents – that is your vocabulary.
- Perhaps you work very slowly – that is your vocabulary.
- Perhaps you're unable to move your right hand – that is your vocabulary.

Wherever you are and whatever you are doing, that is your vocabulary. So pay attention to your limits, or skills, as they will dictate your practice. So many times I've heard artists say, 'I can't do that', as a negative, whereas I think it's a positive, clearly wiping out whole areas of art that they then don't have to be bothered with.

For example, if you don't work well on your own, perhaps your future lies in collaborative practice.

Or you need to pay special attention to networks.

At all times, mine your limits, they are the mainstay of your artwork.

In the early days of your career this self-development work will have to be paid for out of your own pocket. It's very unlikely that an artist or company straight out of university or art school will receive any large-scale subsidy within the first few years of their career.

You need to look like you have tested the work –

- In front of an audience.
- In a public space.
- In a variety of settings.

Developing –

- A style.
- A voice.
- A vocabulary.
- A critical understanding of your own work.

Don't expect a big pay cheque waiting for you every day on your doormat.

- Get another job.
- Get a job with connections.
- Get a job within 'the industry'.

- Get a job that doesn't run contrary to your creative instincts.
- Get a job with broadband, telephone access and a photocopier (that you can use on the side).

Don't rely on art as your sole source of income (it'll create compromises).

- Sell yourself as friendly.
- Sell yourself as reliable.
- Sell yourself as on time.
- Sell yourself as a multi-tasker.
- Sell yourself as around the place.
- Sell yourself as a useful contact.
- Sell yourself as indispensable.
- Sell yourself as you.

The nature of vocabulary is that it is based on your limits, but needs time to grow.

It develops over time. Remember small increments added over a longer period build a practice.

In fact, these steps are the artwork.

Use your limits to define yourself.

The Exercise

Write a list of your limits, or what you currently feel stops you. Perhaps you don't live in a big city? Or you don't have enough time?

Write down ten obstacles.

Then invert them.

Think of the advantage in each one. For example, the advantage in not being in a big city might be that you can paint or describe nature more directly. Or if you don't have enough time, an advantage might be that you have to work instinctively and quickly.

For each of the ten limits find an inversion.

At the end you will have a list of positives that come out of your negative situation. Use these positives to define your own vocabulary.

For example, as above, you can quickly and instinctively paint or write about nature scenes, in the form of haikus or sketches.

This is your practice.

Don't rely on art as your sole source of income (it'll create compromises).

ARTIST'S COMPASS

Use your artist's compass, your intuition, to make radical decisions about your work. In 99% of cases your instinct will be correct.

By artist's compass, I mean a sense that something is wrong, or a feeling in your gut that part of your artistic practice needs to change. Follow your enthusiasms as you might hop on a bus, leading you on a journey of discovery far afield. It's OK. You can always come back.

In the early days of your practice, when you are developing a vocabulary, this might appear difficult, dangerous even. Don't worry. Everything is just paint and words. You can always erase it. In fact you should cultivate your errors, because they will lead you in new directions, into the unconscious, beyond the day-to-day world, into unexplored territory.

Your intuitive artist's compass, and its ability to lead you in unexpected directions, will develop over time.

But here are some clues –

The Exercise

If you are not sure what to do next, simply close your eyes, lie on the floor, or sit quietly and take the question 'What is happening?' inside you.

Bring your attention to a point just below your belly button and breathe into that place.

Take three deep breaths and notice anything that happens, any images or colours that emerge.

Keep breathing until it feels time to come back.

Open your eyes and think about the image that you have seen. What does it tell you about your practice here today?

Repeat often to cultivate your artist's compass.

Often the images that come from this exercise can be included in your work. Use them in your practice in order to make your vision more sophisticated.

Don't question the image. Simply let it exist in the work to add a mysterious and potent quality to your art. Let the work be the interrogation.

By the way, a sign of a great artist is the ability to delete something and start again. Cultivate your willingness to make radical decisions about your own work.

I don't mean just keep it on your desktop and realign it, or change the title. Sometimes you really have to throw something away and completely start again.

Often I've found that right at the end of a long process of making, the work has to be completely destroyed in order to move forward.

The struggle within yourself is the possibility of undoing what has been so carefully and lovingly put together.

- If it's a piece of work, let it flow.
- If it's not working, put it in a drawer and come back to it.
- If it's not working after three years, forget about it.
- If it's really not working after five years, discard it completely. Try a new career.

Top Tip
Take out your most beautiful line, the one you're most happy with and see what happens.

9 times out of 10 it will improve the piece.

Take out your most beautiful line. 9 times out of 10 it will improve the piece.

NO BOUNDARIES

Sometimes when you are starting out, you can also have strategic advantages. It's good to be a beginner, with all the magic that it can bring.

In fact, it's not good to completely understand the form of your work because once you understand the boundaries, your practice can be contained by them.

Not knowing is actually a plus. It means your practice is fluid, still changing.

Your work can cross any boundary. It could be –

- Novel/internet.
- Poem/circus.
- Painting/performance.
- Play/ceramic.

Or any multiple of the above. These hybrids sound good to me – in the 21st century it's the space between different disciplines where new forms can start.

I've always thrown away the manuals and gone instinctively into new areas, trusting that I will make something out of raw and unknown materials. In the 90s I made some work that I was told by other people was 'Performance Art'. So I rode the 'Performance Art' wave until I landed somewhere else – 'Net Art'.

The same thing happened again. I can now see my practice as a series of waves, ongoing. Sometimes chaotic, unknown, tossing me around, until I land somewhere else.

The only realities I know about making artwork are –

- It's difficult.
- It involves the self.
- It involves the unknown.
- It's chaotic.

THE ONLY WAY TO MAKE THE WORK IS TO MAKE THE WORK.

i.e. you will have to process the self, the chaotic, the unknown, in order to make art. This is difficult. Unfortunately that is the challenge – the process of difficulty.

If you want to continue to make art you must accept that there will be difficulty created by making work.

Often we believe that the process of change will only affect our audiences, not ourselves. Actually the impact on us is far greater than on any third parties.

Audiences have choices, they can walk away from a process. You can't.

Top Tip

At the start of a project calculate how much work you think it will take to achieve its aims. Then multiply by three. It will always take much more time, effort and creativity than you can imagine.

Create an invisible moat around yourself that will support you through this period. A network of friends, mentors, colleagues, assistants. Create structures that include time out of work, feedback, evaluation, holidays.

Give yourself the real amount of time you will need to complete your project –

- A month.
- A year.
- Ten years.

Twenty Things To Do To Work With Difficulty

- Accept difficulty.
- Accept you have made a difficult career choice.
- Take difficulty inside you, praise it.
- Bring the difficulty into the work.
- Take difficulty to the supermarket, walk it around, see its choices.
- Imagine the hard surfaces of difficulty, what would happen if they fell away?
- Celebrate success and failure equally.
- Have a party to celebrate not getting that grant.

- Make friends with misfortune, it will help you big time.
- Bring difficulty into the present, into now.
- Slowly fold difficulty inside you as you would an egg in a cake mix.
- Meet difficulty head on. Take awkward phone calls.
- Take responsibility for difficulty. The buck stops with you.
- Tango with difficulty and pleasure, make them twin partners.
- Realise that being an artist is unlikely to make you rich.
- Realise that being an artist is unlikely to make you famous.
- Realise that being an artist is unlikely to make you sexually desirable.
- Accept an ordinary life.
- Accept that things will change.
- Accept that you are extraordinary.

Not knowing is actually a plus. It means your practice is fluid, still changing.

SCRAPS

In times of difficulty, it has sometimes happened to me that there's only one image/idea in my notebook.

If so, then that's where I have to begin.

Remember that you can begin the process of making with –

- One line.
- One note.
- One word.

In fact that's where you have to begin. You are always, inevitably, starting with the blank sheet.

There are twelve dimensions of loneliness within the empty page.

Stop waiting for the great idea, the great grant, the great producer. You begin from here, where you are now. You begin from no space and add letter by letter, word by word until you fill one sentence and then one page.

Address your fear of the empty page.

Here's some space for you to make something out of –

How did it feel?

I once ran a workshop with Susan Rethorst, an American dance artist, at Dartington School of Art. In a writing exercise Susan brought in the idea of 'scrapel'. It's an American word taken from food preparation – after the butchery process, it's what's left on the floor. In essence the scraps. Scrap-el. Out of this material food would have been made. I liked this idea. It stayed with me.

The students had to make something out of scraps. What was left. Not perhaps the great, formidable idea of their dreams, but the isolated images, lines and phone numbers left in their notebooks.

We're always making things out of scraps. I'm always making things out of scraps.

A client was suffering from a bad period of RSI and so she asked me how she should fill in her bursary application because she couldn't type up more than one page of A4. I suggested that since the piece was about shadows, absence, she fill the rest of the pages with her drawings of shadows.

In fact, if she used her RSI hand to hold a pencil, (like using your left hand if you're right-handed) something would come through that would make a statement about where she was. Even if it didn't express itself clearly on the page, it would still speak volumes about her predicament.

- Enjoy the fragments that you have.
- Enjoy them as pure material.
- Use your disadvantage to your advantage.

If you only have scraps, make something interesting out of them – gather together your fragments. You are working to deepen even the slightest materials, even shadows.

Top Tip
Interesting scraps are always better than a polished void.

Use your left hand, if you are right-handed, or vice versa, to access the world of the unconscious, your intuitive process, your gut feeling.

Find out what's really inside you.

You begin from here, where you are now. Word by word until you fill one sentence and then one page.

TELL US HOW IT FEELS

At the bottom of an email to an artist I say, 'Tell us how it feels'.

I mean – your artwork is about feeling. Even if it's not about feeling, it's about the avoidance of feeling. Even if it's abstract art, it's about the space of no feeling.

So in your artist's statement, tell me how it feels.

Is it –

- Sad.
- Lonely.
- Abstract.
- Angry.
- Guilty.
- Energetic.
- Loud.
- Spacey.
- Vulgar.
- Shameful.
- Futile.
- Ugly?

What's the mood? The tone?

Come at your statements from a place of 'I'.

Tell us what you want, how you feel, where this will take you, how it will work for you.

This might seem unnatural to you. Just notice that. If your tone is glacial abstraction, then that is feeling for you.

Instead tell us why you need more of this quality. Or how glacial abstraction could be added to/challenged/ debated. Feeling is what comes from a place of authenticity. What happens when you are really being yourself?

We spend so much of our lives not being who we really are, do you want to spend time in your artwork also doing that?

Twenty Ways To Work With Feeling

- Take your emotional temperature every day.
- Listen to your feelings.
- Each day write a line in your notepad about how you are. Note any subtle shifts or changes.
- Be unashamed about this activity – it's time for you.
- Note the moods and shifts in your process of making.
- Note the moods and shifts in what you are making.
- Note the moods and shifts in what you want to make.

- Watch when you tip over.
- Watch when you are angry.
- Watch when you are euphoric.
- Allow the poetry of every day to seep into your life.
- Don't ban any feeling.
- Don't short circuit any feeling.
- Feeling is not failure.
- Feeling is not fleeting.
- Feeling is not fictitious.
- Let feelings be your best guide in the making of your work.
- Let anti-feeling be your best guide in the making of your work.
- Speak something honestly and with authenticity, including all the good parts and the bad stuff that really happened to you.
- Then you really will have universal art.

Working in this way can take a long time, so don't be disheartened if it doesn't happen all at once. However, working with feelings can add an emotional density to your work that's very attractive to other people.

Start today by writing down twenty adjectives that describe what you're feeling right now.

We spend so much of our lives not being who we really are, do you want to spend time in your artwork also doing that?

IDEAS FOR CASH

When you are in a process of developing a practice
you should not ignore anything that comes to you.
In fact, it's helpful to stimulate ideas from a variety
of sources.

There are many methods for augmenting this kind
of chance process, but here is a great Andy Warhol
technique that I've used all the way through my career.

If I run out of solutions, I ask other people who I trust,
to supply me with ideas that I subsequently pay for.
£1, £10, £100. The amount of cash is up to you and
the limits of your budget.

I am not the only person having good ideas.

- Good ideas are out there, floating on the breeze,
  in the ether.
- Good ideas can be found.
- Good ideas can be hunted.

The useful thing about paying for ideas is that, in a
time of difficulty, it takes you outside yourself, into
a different kind of space and that shock might jolt
you out of the confines of your current logic and make
a change.

For example, asking a whole group of people for £1 ideas might create a piece in itself, quite different from what you had in mind.

- It opens you up to the possibility of collaboration with others.
- It opens you up to the creativity of the universe where solutions can be easily found.

The problem is not with the absence of ideas, the problem is with the level of development of your own radar, your artist's compass – learning how to pick up the best signals rather than a dull monotone drone.

So ultimately the best relationship you can cultivate is with your own universal creator or inner resource bank, whatever you want to call it.

Whilst you get to this happy place, paying out for a few good ideas won't do you any harm.

My only proviso is –

- Choose people with good aesthetic pedigrees.
- Choose people who understand that this is a fun game and not a sign of your paucity of imagination.
- Choose people who have no investment in controlling your own practice.
- Choose people who aren't afraid.

Also the number one rule of paying for ideas is that you don't have to use them.

They feed your creative process, but don't dictate it.

Top Tip
Ask 20 people for £1 ideas. Use that as the basis for a new work.

Twenty Good £1 Ideas

(If you use any of these please pay me £1.)

It's also a useful recap of the book so far.

- Slow.
- Amplification.
- Fast.
- Feeling.
- Scraps.
- Take up space.
- Non-feeling.
- Cell wall.
- Physicalise.
- Sky.
- Random.
- Simple.
- Marks.
- Litter.
- Mistakes.
- Complicated.
- Volume.
- Colour.
- Rearrange letters.
- Steps.

(Note how this list also becomes a piece in itself.)

Good ideas can be found. Good ideas can be hunted.

GROW YOUR OWN ARTIST

If you starve your own artist it can't grow.

OK it can survive for a while, perhaps even years
under all the rubble of regular life – office jobs,
banking, bills to pay, council tax, but like any plant or
organism it can't thrive long term without sustenance.

Grow your own artist.

Plant artist seeds that can be harvested all year round,
providing creative colour every day.

Create a piece that can be added to one line or one
word at a time, building your work like Lego bricks,
in modular form. Don't always think of the big picture,
the highway, where you're heading, look at the
pavement cracks, the clouds, the sky, the colour of
scratches on a passing car.

Rely on small increments of personal accumulation,
just like the brain works, adding node by node. The
big spectacular display is fun and rewarding but not
the only kind of show.

Throw your artist's seeds into gardens, in the manner
of guerilla gardening, at night, when no one is around
and wait for these flowers to bloom.

Cultivate –

- A long term plan.
- A secret budding career.
- A file on your work desktop marked 'Seeds' full of your ideas.
- 10p a day set aside to pay for trips to galleries, artist's catalogues, postcards.

Bring the energy of your creativity into your 'need-to-pay-the-bills' job, or 'my-boss-is-getting-to-me' workplace relationships by –

- Integrating your hidden singing career into the flow of your office day.
- Sitting in front of your computer working with the precision of your performance art.
- Making a play for the many CCTV cameras on your street, or in the underground, gliding past listening to your favourite iPod soundtrack.
- Dancing on the street – who's looking and who cares anyway?

No artistic activity is wasted, however small or seemingly unseen. Its impact on you is forever, held in the body.

Adapt your current life to include creativity when you can, in the holes in the fabric of your life. In cookery, sweeping leaves, telling the time, washing the dishes.

Top Tip
Once a week go to a book shop with a big magazine
department. Browse through the periodicals for free.
You don't need to buy anything. Take it away in your
head. Focus on whatever draws your interest.

This is your weekly practice.

Sometimes this can be as rewarding, if not more so,
than going to a gallery.

Twenty Ways To Grow Your Own Artist

- Buy magazines or collect free postcards.
  Put them out in a line and re-order according
  to colour, size, content, theme.
- Spend one hour with an image.
- Chose one image and then describe it as yourself,
  using the word 'I'.
- Have a day when you look at the world.
- Have a day when you look at the world through
  your fingertips, your ears, the soles of your feet,
  your nose.
- Have a day when you look at the world through
  your open heart.
- Imagine the world through one sense only.
- Take a bus journey to the end of the line and back.
  Take photos.
- Sit in street café and build a narrative about
  everyone you see. Give them names.

- Paint a picture with midnight broken glass.
- Build a sound file with whispers.
- Create a play with no drama.
- Write a symphony for flat tyres.
- Re-order the universe according to secret, hidden principles.
- Then write the novel of that world.
- Build boundaries around your creativity.
- Destroy boundaries around your creativity on a regular basis.
- In your head move your practice to Brazil, China, Australia, Iceland, Venezuela.
- Make something loud.
- Make something that takes up a lot of space.

No artistic activity is wasted, however small or seemingly unseen. Its impact on you is forever, held in the body.

CURIOSITY

Whilst you are developing a practice, a key component in that process is your own curiosity. This might appear obvious, straightforward, naïve. Yet curiosity is a major strategy in developing an individual voice.

- Be curious about your process.
- Be curious about yourself.
- Be curious about your inner state.
- Be curious about your feelings.

Instead of the blunt instrument of just always doing, investigate the open, seductive, fertile realm of curiosity.

- Investigate.
- Make connections.
- Do research.
- Be curious.

Don't try to control, that will be useless. Just –

- Watch.
- Notice.
- Observe.

Think about what being curious would mean for you.

- More time?
- More space?
- More focus?

- More leisure?
- More research?
- More exhibitions?
- More people?
- More life?

Count backwards every day 1000 – 0 and in that time let your curiosity roam.

Creativity is a tool for the reassembling of reality. It doesn't work to deadlines. It needs room to grow and that space can be a place of waiting. We assume that time on a bus, waiting for someone to arrive, a train delayed is lost time. Perhaps it's just the universe telling you that you need to do nothing.

Seek out opportunities for waiting. Be curious. Watch and wait for what is happening. Look for spaces for being yourself.

- The view.
- The park bench.
- The journey by train.
- The queue.
- The office on a slow Friday afternoon.

These are good places to bring your awareness to yourself and anything that brings awareness to your inner self, will encourage your own artist.

Top Tip

Use delays in transportation. Use delays when people don't arrive. Use others' lateness as a way of finding the necessity for stoppages in your life.

Don't resist these gaps, these possibilities for waiting when they arrive.

They are magical moments.

The Exercise

Curiosity is difficult to pin down. However it can easily be conjured up, manifested by doing different kinds of research. This information gathering is central to your practice and should be warmly encouraged.

Instead of making a new piece, make research around it, using your curiosity to look this way and that, from each angle, filling your notebook with ideas.

Rather than making a definitive work out of what you have seen, present the research as the final piece.

Whatever you see on this journey is art.

Use delays in transportation. Use delays when people don't arrive for finding the gaps in your life you didn't know you needed.

WHAT'S INSIDE YOU

- Trust your intuition.
- Trust that what you find is what you need.
- Trust what falls into your lap.
- Trust what is easy.

Everything is in there, inside you, waiting to be discovered. It might take a long time to come out, but it is still there.

All your fantasies about the solutions to your work being out there, beyond yourself, in the form of managers, funders and promoters, are largely delusion.

- Everything is unexpected.
- Come to it for the first time like a child playing.
- Trust the nature of materials – they'll always lead you in the right direction.

As an artist, curiosity is naturally at the heart of your process. It should manifest in the work itself and in how you approach your practice.

Rather than looking to absolutes – blocks of certainty that you manoeuvre around, like walls of a house, use curiosity to make investigations into things, peering through the windows into other kinds of space.

Doorways, corridors, roofs.

When you come up against difficulties in your work, use curiosity as a kind of pass key into another building, somewhere you haven't been before.

- Be curious about your process.
- Be available to process.
- Be curious about your inner state.
- Be available to yourself for investigation.

Curiosity needs time and time is often the one thing that, if you're working to deadlines, you can't allow yourself.

Whatever difficulty you find yourself in within the working process, whether alone or with others, I would invite you to take ten minutes out of your schedule to explore what's inside you –

- Leave the room.
- Find another space that is quiet and still.
- Take some breaths into your abdomen.
- Breathe deeply.
- Go inside yourself – find some inner space.
- See if an image comes.
- Acknowledge that image, note what it means for you.
- Ask the picture why it is here.
- Find a connection with the image and your current process.

Use these steps each time to cultivate your inner space.

- In time you will not need to leave the room.
- In time you will not need ten minutes.
- In time you will be able to look inside you, in the same casual way that you look out of a window.

Under no circumstances allow anyone else in your creative process – collaborators, directors etc, – to enter into your personal creative space for these ten minutes. For this time you are alone, in yourself, being curious, following your intuition.

This is YOU time.

Top Tip
Substitute any feeling – anger, sadness, disappointment – for curiosity about that same feeling, or even its opposite.

Don't deny the feeling, just be curious where it comes from. So, you're disappointed you didn't get the grant/commission/award.

Why does it feel so tough?

Is there something about the hurtfulness that's nothing to do with the grant whatsoever?

Twenty Ways Of Working With What's Inside You

- Describe yourself as a colour.
- Describe yourself as a taste.
- Describe yourself as a country.
- Describe yourself as a number from 1-10.
  1 being freezing cold, 10 being red hot.
- Make this taste, country, number, colour your
  next project.
- Pay attention to reverie, daydreams and absent
  reflection.
- Pay attention to events on the street.
- Give them a symbolic value.
- Fill your whole body up with fire, water, earth,
  air – check the results.
- Get into the body at least once a week – swimming,
  running, yoga etc.
- Make work for the body.
- Make work for the senses.
- Make work for your hands.
- Make work for your feet.
- Make work that has contradictory logic, is awkward,
  backward, difficult, critical.
- Make work that relies on nothing.
- Make work that is free to disappear.
- Make work that can be held in a balloon.
- Make work that can be in the body.
- Make work for one of your cells.

Use curiosity as a kind of pass key into another building, somewhere you haven't been before.

TIME

Give yourself enough time. Don't propel yourself
through a series of hoops, just because you think
you ought to.

Be kind to yourself.

Pay for time and enjoy it.

R & D (Research And Development) = A Minimum Of
Three Months

Perhaps you think you can do this work within one
week. The reality might be that you can only pay
people for one week. If so, go ahead and use the
week, but place it within a longer time frame.
One, two, three months.

Let yourself breathe.

Think about why you are crushing your creativity into
one week. Imagine the pressure building. Like a pot
on the boil with all the steam pouring out of the lid.

If you have to work to deadlines in this way (and
sometimes deadlines are good) at least give yourself
the same amount of time to process the work. So, if
your workshops are for one intense week, give yourself
at least another seven days alone to process the

material from this period. And then perhaps one week with your company to send emails backwards and forwards, to get other feedback.

A Project = A Minimum Of Six To Twelve Months

Don't underestimate how much time something will take you to do.

In budgets, as in projects, as in life, add at least one third to your idea of how long something will take. Be generous to yourself. Who cares when it gets completed as long as it does get finished successfully?

Again, if you can't pay yourself for twelve months within the budget, create a system where you simply pay yourself for a number of weeks over a year. The rest of the time is unpaid. The main thing is to ringfence time, that most slippery of elements.

I've long thought that artists should be able to buy time, as from a shop, just to create process. They ought to go to funders and say, 'I want to buy X weeks of time @ £X per week please.'

Residencies = Twelve Months Plus

Unfortunately most people have a completely unrealistic idea of how long it will take to create a work of art.

The same goes for agencies offering residencies. One, two, three months. They think it can all be wrapped up in that time. The idea of artists' research time is an alien concept to them.

So don't be bullied into making your piece too soon, especially when you do get funding. The pressure will be on from them or from yourself to achieve something quickly. Make sure you protect yourself by having enough time.

I've witnessed many companies making excellent unfunded work, or working with small grants. As soon as they get their first big award they make the worst show of their career.

Once when I was an artist on a major public residency I was called in during the first week by their PR department for images of the piece I was about to make. So be careful, give yourself enough time, don't be bullied, don't be harassed and don't allow yourself to release the work before it's finished.

Top Tip
If a PR agency asks for a selection of images to choose from, only send the images you want to see in print (this is usually one, and at the very most two). Don't be persuaded and cajoled into sending more. Inevitably they will choose the image that you DON'T want to use. If you only send one, they can only choose one.

Research = Life

Time = research = life.

Process is happening all around you. Be observant. You don't need a lot of money to make work. It can be made from a fragment, it can be made now, it can be made alone.

On the street, walking by the motorway, at the supermarket, at the cashpoint queuing, on a train with a notepad, in traffic, outside in a park listening.

Your eyes and ears are free.

Use them.

As always your work can be dramatically changed by its relationship to time. If you are struggling with an idea, slow down to the speed of your heartbeat. Extend the piece to take up the space of an hour, ten hours, twenty-four hours, a week, a lifetime.

A simple task documented every day for the rest of your life might be the epic you have always hoped for.

Your eyes and ears are free.

Use them.

DOING NOTHING

Filling every available space with ideas, words, or process is not the way to get the best out of your creativity.

Take time out –

- Sit in a street café.
- Look out through big glassy windows onto the passersby.
- Detune your eyes.
- Think of one simple idea that will transform your project.

Look into your latte, or cup of tea, for inspiration. It's amazing what you can see when you really look into the frothy surface of your cappuccino.

Sometimes just doing nothing feels like the right thing to do.

In Taoism *wu wei* means doing nothing. *Wu wei* is one of my favourite things. The Taoists believe that doing less, or stopping, just might be the right thing to do.

Wait for things to unfold. Don't force yourself. Step back from your project. Take time off in the steam room and wait for inspiration.

(Well perhaps Lao-Zu, famous Taoist, might not say go to the steam room. Then again...)

I apply this *wu wei* idea a lot to my creativity, believing that overwork is a form of blockage or even psychosis. Doing nothing might actually solve the problem or make you face the difficulty.

Doing nothing is my favourite way of 'working'. I get more done and I am more refreshed after an hour of *wu wei* than days of working, nose to the grindstone, on a new piece.

In fact I've had some of my best ideas whilst in this place of absent reflection.

Big windows = reflection.

Top Tip
Do nothing for one second, one minute, one hour.

After the period is over, write down any struggles you have with the exercise on a paper napkin, then leave it on a café table to be thrown away.

Other good places to do nothing are –

- A park bench.
- Standing in the shallow end of a swimming pool.
- Standing under a shower.
- Watching rice boil.

- Watching paint dry.
- A library.
- A station.
- A sauna.

Experiment with these environments and write to me telling me what you find.

Take time out.
Do nothing.

TITLES

A title can hold the focus, direction and potential
of a piece of work.

Actually a piece of work can simply be a collection
of titles. So, in my own notepad, a page of potential
titles I often see as one coherent work. It's just a
series of texts manifesting in a different way.

Read a page of random notes and lines in your notepad,
as if it were one document.

Imagine that you are at a reading. Stand up and speak
your text out loud.

- What do you notice?
- What's the feeling?
- What do you discover?
- What's the focus of your piece?

Sometimes I find that in a document or piece of
writing, the first line, whatever it is, or how bizarre
it might seem, can become the title.

Look through your notepad, reading the first line
of each page as though it were a title.

I like long titles. I like single words. I like acronyms
as titles.

Sometimes in my own practice, I've had a title a long time before the work was made, in the back of my head, waiting for the right subject to attach to it.

Most people make something and then title it whereas I constellate a particular piece around a title.

Some titles are just too good not to use. Everything is a potential title.

I like the fact that my titles confuse people. '...', 'IMHO', ': (:)' – are all good examples. They see them as mistakes in the sentence. I view the titles as punctures, rather than punctuations in the text.

A title can be an explosion in someone's head, pulling them into a work of art.

- Confuse.
- Intrigue.
- Delineate.
- Pollinate.

If you're writing an application, always give a piece of work a title. Never use 'Work In Progress' or even worse 'Untitled'. Be clear, positive, certain – even if you don't feel that way, give the impression that you know what you're doing.

Nothing is more magnetic than certainty.

The Exercise

Write down ten potential titles on a page. Go away.
Come back. Does the entire page look like a poem,
a text, a first scene, a description of a painting?
If so, keep writing.

Make sure that you keep a lookout for potential
titles everywhere. On the sides of buses, advertising
hoardings, shopping lists, misheard conversations
on the underground.

Alert your artist's antenna to the power of titles
in order to transform your work.

Look through your notepad, reading the first line of each page as though it were a title.

SLOGANS

A slogan is something you can write on a T-shirt
and be happy wearing it.

Slogans are crass, vulgar and good at getting your
work across quickly (subtlety can come later).

I once worked with an artist applying for money as a
theatre director. We came up with the acronym ODP
which stands for Organic Devising Process. OK so
it's stupid, I know. But guess what, he got the money.
And I believe ODP secured it.

Slogans provide a shortcut, a route into your work.

But I hear you complain that your work's about a lot
of things, it can't be reduced to a few neat phrases.
My response would be that if the work is about
complexity, find a way of describing that complexity
in just three words –

ABOUT
CHAOS
THEORY

For that one moment, when you are talking to a
curator or producer, make everything simple.

About my own work I say –

I'M
A
MAGICIAN

Who cares if no one knows exactly what it means?
At least it's an opening gambit. If they ask what that's
about, then I go ahead and explain. If they don't, what
have I lost?

Some made up slogans –

ODP

Simple Vs Complex

YOU +
ME
ART

cooperatingcreativecollaboration (CCC)

The Exercise

Use this space to create your own slogan.

What have you come up with?

Find a way of describing what you do in just three words.

THE FLOWER IS RED

Complexity is what you are aiming for in your arts practice. Complexity and simplicity.

That's why the title of this section is not immediately apparent. That's why the title doesn't appear to have anything to do with the content. Just yet.

I allow complexity to reveal itself.

That kind of discovery is a key feature of complexity.

Allow multiple viewpoints to create a kind of matrix, as in a dream, something partially known, but needing investigation. That would be perfect.

Symbols can create complexity.

Symbols are archetypal extensions of you, like a mechanical arm extending out into creative space, just like one of those grabbing machines that you see in amusement arcades, where you try to win a ring, a soft toy, a watch.

Symbols reach out to audiences at an emotional level, below the frequency that can be usually heard, allowing them to connect with your themes. These symbols can be big or small, mute or loud.

- Dust is a symbol.
- Mother is a symbol.
- World is a symbol.
- Atom is a symbol.

One of my favourite symbols to work with is blue.

A client came in to see me to talk about a project. Part of our work together was to work on a title, to somehow give the piece form, shape, focus, energy, so people could see it.

The project was a radical reinterpretation of a Samuel Beckett play. Off the top of my head I came up with the title 'The Flower Is Red', just as an example, but when I said it, it seemed to fit. I don't know where this title came from, or what it means but for me it was exactly the right one for the piece, absurd, with echoes of clowning, like Beckett's work with Buster Keaton.

I imagine a squirt of water coming out of a toy red flower...

Top Tip
Give your piece a vivid, memorable title. Drop in a colour. Make the name twenty words long.

Grab their attention right from the very first line.

Run against the zeitgeist.

Remember, the zeitgeist is always just about ready
to collapse.

Symbols reach out to audiences at an emotional level, below the frequency that can be usually heard.

THE CHILD PART

In Part Two of the book I have encouraged you to develop your practice, using key concepts like 'Artist's Compass', 'Curiosity', 'Intuition' and 'No Boundaries'. However this always only refers to the child part of yourself that in adulthood becomes damaged and often destroyed.

Discouraged, abbreviated, suppressed, abridged – our creative self gets policed by the sensible, practical world of grownups.

What has happened to your child?

In my office, on my desk, I have kids' toys, ready for adult clients to play with. However, sadly, these rarely get used, as my visitors perhaps don't want to be seen as foolish or immature.

On the other hand, I take any opportunity to get down onto the floor and play with toys. I've long since got over the idea of making a fool of myself.

So a large part of developing a practice is getting in touch again with the freewheeling part of yourself that once held simple objects in awe and wonder – a cardboard box, a piece of string, a spinning glass, a pile of sand.

How much of modern art is a need to get in touch
again with the materials we played with so freely
as children?

Listen to your heartbeat.

- Play with toys.
- Get down on the floor.
- Use materials freely.
- Be in a child place.

And you won't go far wrong.

What has
happened to
your child?

GIVE THEM SOMETHING FOR FREE AND THEY WILL LOVE YOU FOREVER

People like to get something for free.

Give them something to remember you by – a free gift, a postcard, a message, a toy. Do something for free, offer generosity and you will be rewarded tenfold.

If you always take, you will struggle to endear yourself to anyone.

Offer –

- A birthday candle.
- A crisp.
- A tarot reading.
- A jelly baby.
- A manicure.
- A lift.
- A whistle.
- A free drink.
- A piece of cake.

Top Tip
Don't be afraid to make a fool of yourself in order to develop your good nature.

Cool isn't everything.

Do something for free, offer generosity and you will be rewarded tenfold.

3

WORKING
ON YOURSELF

What You Will Learn In This Section

- The value of working on yourself.
- Yourself as a process.
- The beginnings of self-knowledge and empowerment.

I believe that you are the source of your own power.

All of the answers are inside you. Learn to work with your own inner processes, paying attention to all the information that you find there.

Part Three offers a generous approach, allowing you the time and resources to successfully support your own artist's practice.

Move forward dynamically.

VALUE YOURSELF

In the long term, as an art practitioner, one thing that you must learn above all others is the value of yourself.

IF YOU DON'T VALUE YOURSELF NO ONE ELSE WILL.

You won't sell paintings, you won't be invited to make performances, no one will publish your books.

Unless you make yourself seen in this way, occupying the centre stage, your practice will continue, but only at a minor level.

- Occupy space.
- Be unafraid.
- Take risks.
- Charge accordingly.

Who cares what other people think? It's YOU we're talking about here.

This might manifest in a number of ways –

- Using good materials.
- Pricing at market rates.
- Not working for free.
- Paying for necessary equipment.

It's important to invest in your practice, to support yourself. If you need a digital camera, buy a good quality one that will be a pleasure to use, ergonomic and satisfying.

Don't worry if it costs £200 more than the cheaper one. Your feelings of enjoyment will enter the work, making the photographs commensurably better, enlarging your practice.

Don't worry.

Be bold in the support of yourself. If, at the moment, no one else will do that for you, it's imperative that you start to do it for yourself.

- Studio space.
- Accommodation.
- Materials.
- Collaborators.

Also –

- Meals out.
- Travel.
- Books.
- Going to the cinema.

If these fuel your practice, then go ahead and do them.

Don't beat yourself up.

Top Tip

At all times act as though you are successful. This is not arrogance, but expresses a confidence about yourself that is modest and real.

If necessary, put appropriate boundaries around yourself to protect your work.

If you don't value yourself no one else will.

WORK FOR FREE

Conversely, if you're an artist who's been around for a while, it can be very liberating to do work for free. In fact, this paradox, of paying yourself properly and yet on occasion working for no cash, can be a very dynamic position.

If you're caught up in the spell of commissions/funding/clients you can forget the excitement of making your first piece – with no money, no equipment and no demands.

I've found that when I've made some work for free, for myself, something energetically happens, some alchemy occurs. It becomes magnetic. Perhaps it's the enthusiasm or the generosity with which it was made that attracts other people, but it seems to automatically draw an audience.

That audience might be 1 or 2 but what's the problem with that?

In a culture set on automatic to 'making it', especially the art world, it feels good to find someone doing something for free with a genuine passion for creating. That is always going to be infectious.

The company of careerists, cadavers and clowns is not good for your artistic practice, even if it's fun for a while.

To balance your career out sit in Piccadilly Underground Station with a handwritten sign around your neck saying, 'Artist Working For Free – Please Contribute'.

The more successful you are as an artist, the less time you will have to make art. Or the bigger the art will get, with the attendant possibility it will become more abstract and empty.

Keep doing things for free. Who says that these works have to be outputted, or even finished? In a time of stress they might be the only thing in your inbox marked 'Private'.

- Do it on your own.
- Do it but adopt an entirely different name for a week.
- Make it in a different language.
- Create a new alphabet to build it.

Do it for free, keep it private and look at it just for yourself.

Your audience might be 1 or 2 but what's the problem with that?

PARENT AND CHILD

The relationship between the artist and the funder/
curator/gallery/promoter is very similar to that between
parent and child. The parent provides, gives, offers
security, nurtures – the child screams and shouts.

The artist is always looking for validation, 'Look at me.
Over here. No, me.'

Often the need for validation gets loaded onto the
funder. So the process of applying for money or
getting a promoter to see your work immediately
becomes about so much more.

Nothing to do with the quality of the work at all.

- 'They don't like me.'
- 'I'm not good enough.'
- 'They don't want to support me.'
- 'X is their favourite artist.'

In an art world that's difficult and strenuous – poor
pay, inadequate housing, few kinds of outputs/
showings – artists need these kinds of narratives,
'They hate me', 'I hate them', just to keep going,
to keep making work.

That these narratives aren't necessarily true is beside
the point. We need them to survive.

However, an acknowledgement that there are these other kinds of stories circulating in your life might give you the edge in developing your art career.

- Be an adult.
- Don't allow yourself to be seen as a wilful child – arrive on time for appointments, come prepared.
- Pay for yourself.
- Offer to take 'them' out for lunch.
- Wash occasionally.

It's shocking how badly artists present themselves.

I've had numerous occasions when young, emerging artists don't turn up for appointments, arrive forty minutes late, don't apologise, don't take any notes, don't arrive with any paper – the list goes on.

It sounds funny, it sounds 'punk rock' but it isn't. It's just irritating. It makes me think of them as not capable. If I was giving out money, or commissions, or residencies, I wouldn't bank on them.

If you want to be 'punk rock', go play in a rock band. If you want to be angry, go rob a bank. If you want to be seen as an adult, behave like one.

'But, hold on,' I hear you say, 'You told us that the child is necessary to who we are as artists – surely that's a good thing? From a place of play, of non-judgement, of lack of boundaries, good things can come. A whole career can emerge. Aren't the funders always encouraging us to cross boundaries, hybridise, make inter-disciplinary work, collaborate with other forms? How can we do this if we don't play, don't throw the soap around a little?'

I would answer, 'Remember that you can play. You also have the power to create. You can be adaptable. You can take on different roles and responsibilities.'

If you want to play at being responsible, you can – it's just another side to your infinitely varied character. Like a diamond, or a spotlight, you can shine this way, then that. You can play at being both parent and child.

Try some of these as characteristics –

- Be calm.
- Don't be angry.
- Listen.
- Don't waste your time or others'.
- Don't hurry.
- Be clear.
- Meet deadlines.
- Be organised.
- Offer boundaries.
- Use spellcheck.

As you step in and out of these sometimes contradictory roles, it's possible that you could find you are good at some of them. In the process, you might even step across the boundary and become the funder, like I have done. See what it feels like on the other side.

- Try out the shoes.
- Sit behind the chairman's desk.
- Play with the fountain pen.
- Swivel the rotating chair.

See – there can be play on the other side. Parents can be players too.

- Remain flexible.
- Be curious.
- Allow yourself manoeuvrability.

Be the parent who looks after your own creative child. Nurture the child, allow it the best possible space.

The Exercise

Rehearse your face-to-face meetings with the funders. Use another artist to sit opposite you. Sell your project. Change roles and listen to their pitch. Then feedback.

What felt positive?
What felt difficult?

Be the parent who looks after your own creative child.

GENEROSITY

Recently I was reading a book of Shunryu Suzuki's talks 'Not Always So' when I was struck by one thing. At the end of each short lecture he says, 'Thank you very much'.

It reminded me of something I saw when I was in Japan, staying at Nishijima's Dogen Sangha, a Buddhist temple in Tokyo. On the door there was a handwritten note which read 'Everybody welcome'.

In Buddhism it's what is called Big Mind. A generosity towards everything. If you have this Big Mind, you treat all things with respect. Since these things seemingly 'out there' are also yourself, you are also treating yourself with respect.

Generosity might manifest in your practice as –

- Paying people properly.
- Giving up your time to work on others' projects.
- Understanding the value of what you have created.

In the early part of my career I never stopped to value anything I did. I just continuously ticked things off a list, never pausing to think about what I had really done.

I now see that as a mistake.

I never celebrated anything that I achieved.

If you never stop and are always feeling overworked, your instinct might be to blame other people, i.e. 'My boss/editor/supervisor/clients are pushing me so hard' but that's rarely the actual source of aggravation. It's likely to be your need, your ambition, your persistence, your ego pushing you forward.

Overwork = your ambition.

Instead, some ways of being generous towards yourself might be –

- Giving yourself enough time to complete a project.
- Paying yourself properly.
- Blocking in your own holidays in your diary at the start of the year and not deviating from this schedule.

Or insisting on a launch each time that celebrates the work that you have done. Ideally this should be public, but if there aren't funds to do this, it's imperative that you personally celebrate before moving on to the next project.

- Take holidays between projects.
- Take days off.
- Go to the cinema.
- Eat ice cream.
- Everybody welcome, even you.

Top Tip
Don't take on projects purely for cash, however much they pay.

Twenty Ways To Be Generous To Yourself

- Pay yourself properly.
- Don't work for free.
- Don't fill your calendar with work just for the sake of it. Be curious about why you do this.
- Give yourself holiday pay and use that money to buy flights, hotels, perfume.
- Give yourself enough time to properly unpack your work, i.e. don't rush straight into the next project without any intervening time. You will eventually burn out.
- Celebrate the end of projects, even if there's no obvious outputs. Throw a party for your colleagues and friends.
- Celebrate success and failure – both will move you forward in equal degrees.
- Invest in the presentation of your work. Frame it well, put money into good publicity materials, choose excellent collaborators. How you exhibit the work says a lot about the kind of value you place on it.
- Sometimes it's necessary to pay for meals – for yourself and others. Invite the curator/funder/promoter out for lunch.
- Budget realistically for time/costs/resources. Calculate your time in hours.

- Fix your fee, then add another third.
- Have a rate card, or figures to hand, for any eventuality, or job.
- Think seriously about pricing.
- Be prepared to negotiate downwards. However take care not to set too low an initial fee or the client will debate the amount and then you'll be left working on a job that doesn't pay properly.
- Don't be afraid of turning down work if conditions don't feel right. If it feels appropriate to do so, tell the client your reasons.
- Learn to say 'No'.
- Learn to say 'No' with confidence.
- Give appropriate boundaries around your personal life. For example, don't take work calls after a certain time of day. Ring them back tomorrow.
- Don't check your work emails after 6pm.
- Create a good balance of work and play. Don't overwhelm yourself every day – it's not productive. One of the best things you can do is go disco dancing on a Saturday night – it will release energy across the whole of your week.

Once an artist came to see me. We talked about taking the work seriously. This might mean spending more money – on paper, materials, workplace.

For him that meant the difference between a bike costing £100 and another, a better model, at £190.

If these are items that you use every day, you need to invest in them, as each amount of money spent will enhance your life, your practice.

Sometimes spending money can be good energy.
It means that you value yourself, your own life. This permeates through to the work. If you invest, more money will come back. Also, how can you ringfence the work, and so set good pricing, if you don't set good financial boundaries around yourself?

This might manifest on the most basic level as buying a coat, a flat, a pair of jeans, a bike.

Be generous with yourself and it will come back tenfold.

Take holidays between projects. Take days off.

GO WHERE THE ENERGY IS

This lesson has been learnt by me through hardship and personal difficulty. So I give it to you as a big gift – go where the energy is.

Go where you feel comfortable, where there is generosity, where there is hope and concern for your well-being. Go to people you feel comfortable with and who like you. Don't go towards people who don't like you. You sometimes believe that you can convert them. You can't. Steer clear.

Once I was told by a colleague to put a well known curator on my mailing list. I didn't really have a good feeling about this. My intuition was right – the first time I sent out a mail shot, advertising a recent exhibition, she asked to be unsubscribed. I immediately took her off the list.

Ten years later, knowing that she had recently given out grants to artists working in similar ways to myself, it was again suggested that she would be a useful contact. However I still had the previous experience in mind. I wondered what I should do? Even though my instinct told me not to try, I did write to her. And guess what? She told me my work couldn't be funded under her programme.

It wasn't perhaps that she didn't like me or my work but, as I realised many years previously, the energetic exchange was bad. I didn't get the money, but what was worse, I wasted a lot of my own good energy on a bad situation.

It was a big learning experience for me.

The reality is if you don't get a good feeling from a person, a curator, or an institution, don't go near them. You're probably right. It's likely to be a mismatch. You will only frustrate yourself. Ignore them, avoid them and only talk to them if they approach you.

Stay in your own good space and be yourself.

Your peace of mind is more valuable that any seductive idea of fame/money/celebrity.

The carrot at the end of the stick usually turns out to be rotten and full of worms. Buy your own carrots – fresh, organic and full of life.

I have never got a job, or a paid commission, or a residency through any speculative approach.

Only relationships make things happen. I find that the connections that are useful to me aren't in far-flung places, where I don't have any real contact, they're much closer to home. In fact usually right under my nose.

If you are looking for a partner, funder, collaborator or host – look local.

Most of the clients who come to see me find that their support structures are already there, close to home. Plus, because they have evolved naturally, they are usually rock solid, with very good energy.

- Ask your friends.
- Ask your friends' flatmate/boyfriend/partner.
- Think of all the conversations you've recently had about your work. Who seemed interested?
- Where did you last work for free? Who organised that?
- Make a list of support structures already in place. Organise some meetings.
- Whose direct number do you have?
- Where did you work as a volunteer?
- Where did you study?

Learn to trust the instincts that are part of you –

- Learn to find the meridian of good energy inside you.
- Learn to like helping yourself.
- Learn to avoid the bad energy that saps your creativity.
- Learn to like people who like you.

Learn to trust your instinct. It's always right.

Learn to trust your instinct. It's always right.

THE US AND THEM WALL

Sometimes we don't want to be successful.

If it seems strange that we might unconsciously seek
out failure, in order to protect ourselves – think about
it. It's not such an odd idea.

The 'Us and them wall' is something we all use as
artists to separate us from the possibility that our
work might be realised, might find a focus, might
find a home.

By 'Us and them wall' I mean a kind of satisfaction
that we are different from 'them', whoever 'they' might
be – funders, promoters, curators, administrators. It's
a useful device for keeping us in a particular place.

Many of us have used the 'Us and them wall'.

'They' want us artists to do certain things that we
certainly don't want to do, or are poorly equipped
for, like –

- Filling in applications.
- Doing budgets.
- Making pitches.
- Being an administrator.

Can you hear yourself saying quite aggressively 'That's not what I do. I just want to write/paint/perform/etc.'

That feeling is the 'Us and them wall'.

The 'Us and them wall' doesn't allow 'me' the possibility of also sometimes becoming 'them', of moving fluidly between where I am and where I want to go, of occupying the centre ground.

The 'Us and them wall' is a successful way of not getting what we want and as long as there is that barrier between a false 'us' and a false 'them', it's unlikely that we will achieve our goal of being successful.

The 'Us and them wall' is something that is not physical, it's internal and it's not necessarily connected with what we see or meet. It often comes from a long way back. It can be the voice of censure – perhaps of a parent, or partner. It gets projected onto the things that we meet, often funding bodies or authorities.

Do you come up against the 'Us and them wall' in any other areas of your life?

Write here if you can think of some.

Of course the 'Us and them wall' is not just one way, it's a two way process. The funders (or the family, or the establishment, or society, or big organisations, you can probably substitute any words – see how it works?) can perpetuate an 'Us and them wall', a mentality that doesn't want to have a dialogue with the constituency that they support.

Ever not had your calls returned? Or a 'not eligible' reply for funding? Or felt not seen?

That's the 'Us and them wall' working in reverse. Like looking through a telescope the wrong way, it's a distancing mechanism, designed to keep the high ground at the top of the castle. But essentially it's the 'Us and them wall' working very efficiently.

So having recognised that the 'Us and them wall' might exist, how can you work with it to ensure that you can successfully realise your projects?

First, be aware that it's there – that's all. To allow the possibility to enter your consciousness and to give it space to breathe.

Second, talk to one close friend or other people about the 'Us and them wall' and explore some ideas of how it manifests in your life, being always cautious of only going as far as you want.

Third, be aware when you talk to funders, promoters or administrators of your fear, your need to build the wall.

- What is precious?
- What needs to be protected?
- How can you best protect it?
- What would be your worst fear or fantasy?

Top Tip
In any meetings with funders use only 50% of your normal conversation.

Because you will be nervous, you'll tend to talk a lot and speed up. Slow down and say less.

Let them talk.

Intervene only when necessary.

In any meetings
with funders
use only 50%
of your normal
conversation.
Slow down and
say less.

Let them talk.

A DAY WITHOUT MONEY

This is a self help book that does what no other manual does, it advises you to earn less.

When I first went to the Zen Buddhist temple in France, I'd been told that the location of the site was close to a small village. What I didn't realise was that it was only a small collection of houses and contained almost nothing – a bar, a hairdressers, a butchers. All shut. Nothing else. No cashpoint. Since I hadn't brought enough money with me to cover my stay at the temple, I paid what I could and promised to settle the remainder when I could get a lift to a nearby town.

Unfortunately that left me with nothing – not a penny. Not that I really had any use for money. There was nothing to buy anyway. But the fact of being penniless made me strangely defenceless.

The Exercise

Pass one day in the outside world without spending any money.

Use your creativity to find out what's important to you.

Develop your resources to find things for free.

On this day pay attention to your needs.

This exercise reminds me of the film *E.T. The Extra-Terrestrial*.

I've always thought that this movie has a powerful message about human creativity. In his attempt to 'phone home', E.T. uses an unconventional array of low-tech tools – a length of wire, a kid's Speak and Spell, a wheel from a bicycle, an old radio. With these objects he sends a message beyond the Earth's orbit into outer space.

As an artist I always start from zero. I have nothing. I take disassociated objects and recontextualise them. I send a message beyond the stars. I charge up my field with human electricity. I have everything – but I get there with my own resources.

Going to a Zen temple is a bit like going to the stars – you can get there with no money at all.

Top Tip
Use your eye for the irrational to cultivate an original way of seeing.

In order to build this into your daily life, make one risk choice a week. This might be as simple as choosing a different item on the menu at your favourite restaurant or taking an alternative route to work.

Find one visual item a week (even if you are a writer) to put on your mood board.

Once a month dial a telephone number at random and speak to the person as if you were a –

- Market researcher.
- Requesting information for train timetables.
- Calling for a pizza.
- An astronaut.

Use your eye
for the irrational
to cultivate an
original way
of seeing.

WHY DO YOU DO IT?

If you are strongly and persistently attracted to the funding system, it's likely that you will be driven by injustice in some form or another. Whether you like to admit it or not, this place of not getting what you want, or feeling futile and angry, seems strangely familiar. Like a magnet you're attracted to the punishing relationships of the art world in an unconscious echo of what happened in your family or school.

It sounds too simple to be true but in 9 artists out of 10 I'll show you someone acting out in their art relationships the unequal and often punitive relationships of their childhood. Otherwise why would we persistently come back and grab the short straw – low pay, poor conditions, no career structure, little social mobility, no perks.

When you write it down in a line like this, it sounds pretty grim.

Interestingly one artist told me that the problems generated in her social circumstances were because she had naïvely believed that in her art she could work through the life issues that she needed to address. I was surprised because in her performances she seemed to be doing just that. Strong, empowered, bold, radical – her practice tackled social and racial inequality. I was shocked when she told me that she'd hit a brick wall when she realised that her art wasn't really processing these issues. It was only dealing with them on a surface level.

Likewise I thought I'd addressed family issues. All the audiences I performed to thought that I had as well and loudly applauded my fearlessness. But it was only years later that I adequately dealt with them.

You don't necessarily need to spend hours in the therapy room – although it might help. But be aware that the issues informing your art will get projected onto your relationships and the people you're applying to for money.

Unless they're very clever, the funding bodies are not automatically aware of this, so don't worry, you don't have an arrow pointing to your head saying 'loser'. But your advantage is that you can now, after reading this, become aware of it, train yourself and so use this power to advance yourself.

Like a good card dealer, you can adopt a more advantageous position.

In your interactions carefully notice how quickly feelings come to the surface. Be aware of what they are and note them down. Don't go with your first reaction, especially if it's anger, but be prepared to say, 'I'll take that away and think about it'. It's perfectly professional to say that. I use it all the time.

In meetings promote yourself positively but consciously hold something back. Be passionate, then step away to see what it feels like.

Be natural, fresh, alive, as if coming to this material for the first time. Enthusiasm is highly infectious. Be aware of your body reactions and your breath. Hold yourself well and with dignity. Let everything flow from you and towards you.

You have the power.

This is a lifetime's work, so don't expect miracles. But experiment, play, have fun, be engaged. You will get a reputation for someone who can both talk and listen. If you're talking 100% of the time, you're on the wrong track.

Also remember if you apply for money and get turned down, it's not personally about you.

Many good applications get turned down, for lots of reasons, usually a general lack of cash from the funders.

Don't take it back on yourself and punish yourself for your 'failure'. Or worse still, get angry and lose the confidence of the person your were dealing with. It's also not about them.

It's about the process.

Remember people giving out cash are human beings as well (as much as it fuels your anger to think that they are not).

If your fury reaches burning point, remember that they –

- Have children.
- Have mortgages.
- Have marital problems.
- Have difficult journeys to work.
- Also hate the rain.

(This also works for agents, promoters, galleries, publishers etc.)

As much as it adds to your advantage to demonise them, it won't help you. Unless you accept some of the blame and stop pushing it out on to someone else, you won't advance.

This is a lesson very hard won by me, so take note of what I say.

Top Tip
Process your fears, angst, demons outside your artwork.

If you insist on working through this material in a public forum, that's OK, but get a good therapist.

See them every week.

If you apply for money and get turned down, it's not personally about you.

INTUITION

Intuition is your artist's compass, leading you where you want to go.

Trust your intuition, even when everyone around you is telling you something different. If you don't trust it and get in a mess, try to learn from your mistakes.

- Intuition can be cultivated.
- Intuition can be learnt.
- Intuition is neither masculine nor feminine.
- Intuition is inside all of us.

10 times out of 10 your intuition will be right.

I was going to start this part by suggesting some ways of developing your intuition but at this point I drew a blank. Intuitively I knew what to do but I didn't see how I could explain that to you. So I decided to use the *I Ching* to find an answer.

The *I Ching* is an ancient Chinese form of divination, used for telling the future. I use it in a different way, to tell me about what's happening now, in the room, or what's inside me.

C.G. Jung used this method when writing the introduction to Richard Wilhelm's famous translation of the *I Ching* . He questioned the Oracle about itself, asking the book how he could present its ideas to the

Western mind. The *I Ching* answered with hexagram number 50. *Ting*, meaning the cauldron, suggesting that it was a container for spiritual nourishment.

Since this worked for Jung, I decided to ask the Oracle a question of my own. Q. 'How can we develop intuition?' I used the modern method, throwing 2p coins, then adding up the scores, slowly building up the hexagram on paper, line by line. Finally the reading that emerged was number 52. *Ken*, meaning 'Keeping Still, Mountain'.

This seemed very accurate to me.

My interpretation is that intuition is the mountain inside us, it's our certainty. It lets us go, it brings us back. It's our flowing solidity. It can be called upon by keeping still, by coming back to our mountain place. Being solid inside ourselves. Intuition keeps us firm, grounded, earthed – just like a mountain.

MMMMMMMMMMMMMMMMMMMMMM

(A mountain range.)

So intuition comes from the self, some part of you beyond the ego. It's your artist's compass pulling you into the deeper levels of reality. Use it.

However it's not necessary to throw the *I Ching* in order to access intuition in your work.

Process is everywhere.

It's in your vision, just behind your eyes when you close your eyelids. It's on the street in a pattern of falling leaves on the pavement. It's in spilt paint. It's seen in shifting clouds in the sky, or a flock of birds.

- It's in graffiti.
- It's in animals – particularly birds.
- It's in rain.
- It's in dusk.

And becomes more visible at twilight.

When you learn to 'see' process, you can find it everywhere.

- Some call it magic.
- Some call it personal power.
- Some call it human psyche.
- Some give it no name because it can't be named or owned.

The *I Ching* is simply a conduit for that energy. If we had to name it, we could call that energy 'universe' or 'creativity' or even 'God' – but we don't have to give it any cosmic appellation to see it or even use it.

The *I Ching* questioner, the psychiatrist analysing Rorschach inkblots, even the Zen master calligrapher are all drawing on universal processes.

At one of my recent talks I met a visual artist. She admitted that she saw the kinds of internal pictures I was describing in my lecture but she wasn't able to translate them into her art. I believe that she needed more confidence, more practice in working with images - making them concrete, noting them down.

It's useful to keep a notepad of 'inner images'. Update it regularly. Every month or so look back and see any patterns exhibited there. You'll be surprised at what you find.

Perhaps everything you see is blue. Or only animals are present. Perhaps you see a feeling. Or pictures of a bell.

Remember how useful these images are. They are pouring directly out of your unconscious without end, day and night.

Even if you choose to ignore them and don't pay attention, they will still be present every day of your life, in your dreams.

Top Tip
Keep a digital camera with you, in your pocket, the cheapest kind, for things you see every day (sometimes these now come free if you buy a computer package from high street shops).

Record images in the persona of –

- A stranger.
- An angel.
- A housewife.
- A demon.
- An aeroplane.
- An ant.
- A cloud.

Also –

Develop intuition and chance by using dice to determine decisions in your artistic practice, for example the use of colour.

Use the dice authoritatively and without any hesitation. Even if it seems a crazy choice, do it and see where it takes you. 'Yellow' as a colour might seem the wrong choice, but at some level it's right and you need to follow the 'yellow path' as far as it will take you, even if it turns out to be a dead end.

Instructions: write on a piece of paper a list of possibilities, then throw the dice to make a choice.

Some examples:

Let 1 = Yellow.
Let 2 = Blue.
Let 3 = Orange.

Let 4 = Green.
Let 5 = Pink.
Let 6 = Red.

Let 1 = Make it bigger.
Let 2 = Slow down.
Let 3 = Miniaturise.
Let 4 = Take a break.
Let 5 = Turn it upside down.
Let 6 = Time to stop.

It's very important that you accept the first decision that comes. Don't question it. Don't let your rational mind intervene.

Just do it.

Intuition is your space as an artist to be you, to empower yourself. Intuition is a space for your inner artist.

The Exercise

Sit in a calm, quiet room with no TVs or computers.

Take three deep breaths.

Focus inside yourself, letting all the cares of the day slip away. Bring your attention to the space behind your eyelids.

See if there's an image there. Accept the first picture that you see, however bizarre or unacceptable to you. Even if it's a jumble of images, incoherent, dark, mysterious.

Even if it's colour, a feeling, too bright, invisible, just allow it.

Reflect on this image.

- What is it saying about your life?
- Does it have any impact?
- What qualities are present in the image?
- Are they useful to you?

Try to do this exercise every day or as often as you can.

Intuition = curiosity = creativity = art = life.

Twenty Ways To Encourage Intuition

- Make choices based on instinct.
- Trust your first response, your gut reaction.
- If you get stuck in your head, ask your body what it wants to do/where it wants to go.
- Ask your fingers, hand, hips, feet. Ask your heart.
- Make choices based on the toss of a coin but stick to the results.
- Use the *I Ching* to help access intuition.

- Write and record your dreams. Look for patterns there.
- Keep a notepad/mood board. Look for patterns there.
- Read tea leaves. Look for patterns there. I'm serious. Everything can be a door to intuition.
- Put titles in a hat and pull one out but stick to the results.
- Use automatic writing. Simply begin with a blank page and write for five minutes without pausing or thinking. Take the results seriously.
- Do the Rorschach ink blot test.
- Draw ideas rather than think them.
- Intuit ideas rather than think them.
- Get off the computer and work on the floor.
- Get off the handheld device and use a pen and paper instead.
- Use touch.
- Write poetry.
- Get into the body – swimming, running, cycling.
- If you don't have intuition, pay an expert to develop it with you. This dialogue might stimulate your own intuitive processes.

Make choices based on the toss of a coin but stick to the results.

FEEDBACK

Failure is the best thing that can happen to you.

Without failure there's no way to grow, no way to make changes, no way to learn. Every day, thank your lucky stars that you have the capacity to fail. As an artist it's the single most useful quality you can cultivate.

You didn't get the grant, you lost the commission, you came second in the job interview? Great! You can now really get somewhere...

If I am unsuccessful, I now –

- Regroup.
- Ask for feedback.
- Ascertain whether the energy in the situation is good for me.
- Decide to reapply/refrain.

The most important of these skills is asking for feedback. It can be useful in several ways –

- It can put you in a position of power.
- It can make the funder/curator take you a lot more seriously.
- It can enhance your professionalism.
- It can create an extended dialogue.

If you can learn to ask for feedback it can be a powerful tool in your arsenal.

If possible have a meeting and ask for feedback in person.

If so –

- Keep it brief.
- Keep it to the point.
- Keep it impersonal.
- Don't bring feelings into it.
- Don't bring your sense of failure/anger.
- Keep it cool, dispassionate.

Remember to take notes. Write down their feedback word for word, although your note taking should not impede your involvement in the conversation. Be fully engaged.

In a high-pressured situation, note taking is very useful. It also demonstrates to the person you are meeting that you are serious, committed, professional.

Allow space for the other person to speak. Especially if it's telephone feedback. In stressed situations you will have the tendency to fill all gaps in the conversation. Hold back, speak less, give more space, let them talk. If you're especially nervous, take a friend or advocate, as a witness or scribe.

Get a sense of the energy of the feedback. Was it hurried/leisurely or abrupt/casual? This can tell you a lot about the potential for future applications.

Does the person give good quality feedback?

Is it useful/irrelevant or lively/pretentious? Again that's useful information. Don't comment on this. Just observe, take it in, then process later.

Most artists don't ask for feedback. They get a rejection letter, turning down their application, then mentally switch off, or get very angry. Feedback can give you a sense of closure on your anger, or allow you to put it into a wider context.

For example, there could be 244 applications and only 3 grants offered. Under these circumstances, it's tough that you didn't get chosen, but you can perhaps afford to be a bit more stoical.

Similarly if the feedback from the funding organisation is very poor, or non-existent, if might tell you useful information about them. If they are distant or not engaged with you in a real way, it could be time for you to move on.

Treat this kind of information like gold – it'll take you right into the unconscious of the funder.

Be smart, be observant, be curious, be engaging.

At a feedback session it's also useful to ask some questions –

- Ask open questions, i.e. ones that don't have a 'Yes' or 'No' answer.
- Ask them about their history.
- Ask them about their tastes.
- Ask them about what they have recently funded.

Also –

- Invite them to your show/performance/exhibition.
- If you see them out at an event say 'Hello'.

Some Tips About Funding

- One failed application, that's OK.
- Two failed applications, ask for detailed feedback.
- Three failed applications, question yourself if this is an appropriate agency for you to work with. Ask to have a face-to-face meeting.
- Four failed applications, stop making approaches to them. They won't be funding you.

If you are successful that's great. It's also good to make a little ceremony to celebrate failure, or the shadow side of your success.

Allow both success and failure to have equal space in your life, or equal potential.

If you are overwhelmed and blasé about your success it's certain that failure will be lurking somewhere, ready to trip you up.

Failure is the best thing that can happen to you.

Say thank you to failure when you can. Burn a candle, offer a drink, or a pack of cigarettes. You never know when you might need it.

But I'm also wondering about the need to ask for feedback. Is it seeking praise/validation/support through a different route? Search inside yourself and be honest – is the only feedback that you'd like to get positive?

If so, it'd be helpful not to put yourself in a place where you receive public feedback from uninformed sources – a comments book, an after show discussion, a message board. If you're looking for praise, these can be very damaging forums. The feedback can come too soon, when you're not ready, not at a time in your life when you are able to receive challenging opinions about your work.

IT'S OK NOT TO RECEIVE FEEDBACK AT ALL.

To echo one of those 80s anti-drug TV campaigns 'Just Say No!' If you feel that you can't take feedback, you won't be thought of as less than anyone else.

As artists we all receive criticism for our work, no one is exempt. It's perfectly acceptable to remove yourself from the source of pain.

Just leave the building.

Recently it's become more acceptable in our culture to live with feedback and criticism – it's embroidered itself into our lives. As artists we present earlier, show more work-in-progress, have more artist's talks. The classic finality of the auteur, the grandeur of the definitive statement is less present. Work is generally smaller, more tentative. Feedback is seen as an essential part of the artistic process. I hear more and more about work that uses audience feedback as material for the artistic process.

It becomes less and less acceptable to refuse feedback.

However at some point, as an artist, you will have to let these other voices fade away. You will need to ignore the opinions of others and stand by the statement that you want to make.

Some Tips For Ignoring Feedback

- Don't go to your own openings.
- Don't ask family, colleagues, or even friends what they think.
- Don't apply for public funding.

- Allow only one minute of feedback per person and time them with a stop watch.
- Allow only written feedback on postcards.
- Don't read your reviews.
- Don't talk to the press.

I'm joking but...

Make work that is authentic, centred in you, free of fear, clear, its head so full of energy that it will be difficult to challenge. If you're in that place, negative feedback won't get through to you.

Feel your feet on the ground. Physically place your feet there. Be in the central ground of your being and you won't be shaken. Be a mountain. Be a rock.

On the other hand, receiving feedback is a real skill, almost as challenging as making the work itself. So –

Some Tips For Receiving Feedback

Only accept feedback from those whose aesthetic you value. Otherwise, understand that you open yourself to maverick and possibly valueless opinions.

Set a time limit for feedback – for example no more than two/five/ten minutes per person. It's good to set a boundary. When the time's up, draw your session to a close.

Listen to the feedback without comment. Don't try to protest/challenge/debate.

Take the feedback away, then discard what's not useful. If it's all useless, throw it out.

Put yourself in the other person's shoes. Imagine what their life/relationship/journey to work is like. This might help you to understand the nature of their feedback. Again just listen, don't argue, but later use your curiosity to analyse the situation.

Make notes. The act of writing will help to concretise some of the ideas in the session.

Understand that you have your own agenda for asking for feedback. It may be validation, it could be the need for praise, it might be that you usually feel unheard by others. All of this content will feed into the way in which you receive feedback.

Try and be mindful of your own process.

In a 60 minute meeting don't talk for 59 of those minutes, leaving no room for feedback. The conversation should move backwards and forwards, with a natural flow. Always allow space for the other person.

Feedback can be a great gift. From the right source good advice can considerably advance your practice.

Take care to choose a good person from whom to receive this.

The best and most famous artists are not necessarily the best people to give good feedback. Choose someone who has a developed history of offering advice.

Top Tip
When receiving feedback always keep your feet placed firmly on the ground.

Failure is the best thing that can happen to you.

DRAW YOUR DAY

If your daily life feels like a grind, pulling you in all directions – jobs, children, money, clients – a good way of transforming your time and putting more creativity into your routine is to draw your day.

Take an A4 sheet of white paper, nothing special needed, just a piece of standard photocopy paper and a pencil.

For each activity that you will be doing during the day, place a small picture on the page. Don't worry about your ability to draw – that isn't the point of this exercise. I find that a small symbol will usually do to suggest the feeling of an activity. For example a box with a triangle on top as a house, a crude drawing of a car, stick people for adults and children, a line for a road, a circle in a square for a TV.

Draw all the episodes in your day, both the good and bad, the chores and the pleasures. A wire basket for supermarket shopping, a glass to suggest a party. Use your imagination. Don't worry about making an accurate representation. Do it quickly and energetically.

Put down on the paper the tasks that you will need to accomplish. If you have a crowded day these drawings or symbols might fill the whole page. That's OK.

Take the paper out with you.

As you travel through the day doing each individual activity, rub out the drawing with an eraser (I suggest a pencil with a rubber at the tip). At the end of the day, the paper should be empty again, clear of all activity.

Then throw the paper away and with each day start a new piece afresh.

If you don't complete all the activities, still throw the paper away.

If you find that, with some regularity, you are leaving some drawings on the paper, unaccomplished, then this is perhaps a sign to you that there's some material here that you need to address.

See it as a challenge to put less in your day.

Be creative with this exercise. For example, a building I regularly visit has a small canal next to it, full of wildlife. Every time I draw this location, I find myself adding a swan and a bridge, both realistic features of the site, but not necessarily directly attached to my activity.

Over time these transformative symbols, the swan, the bridge merged with the location, allowing me to think in a new way about my time spent in the building, changing what were often difficult visits into something different.

This exercise is a good way of beginning to work with symbols, making dynamic connections between different elements in your life. It's a probe deep into yourself, looking for clues to your inner process. A bit like sending a bucket down into a deep well, seeking out water.

Remember the pictures that you drew as a child at school? The sun so bright, an inviting path curling over a hill, people under a deliriously blue sky, bright green leaves. A mother or a moon, a train to another town.

Remember how much fun it was to draw these pictures?

The sky seemed so full of life, of potential – the dreams that your current job/partner/client/family appear to crush.

See this drawing exercise as a way of getting in touch with that joyful potential. Make these drawings every day to improve your emotional health.

Top Tip
Get some party balloons in plain bright colours and with a black marker pen write in bold letters all the problems that you are having with your practice –

- Stuck.
- No Money.
- No Freedom.
- Blocked.
- Angry.
- Lost.

(Choose your own words, these are just some suggestions.)

Let the balloons go, off into the sky and with their flight, allow your problems to fly free, to dissolve, to change, to move away.

Watch them until they disappear.

Or stick a pin in and make them go 'pop'.

Make drawings every day to improve your emotional health.

HOW TO END

Since this book began with 'How To Start' it feels appropriate to finish with 'How To End'.

Sometimes it feels as if we just don't know how to end a project.

It can go on for a year, three, five years, ten. The difficulty is that, with a ten year project, it comes to contain all the things that have emerged in that period – all the hopes, all the fears. It becomes emblematic of our struggle.

It usually contains too many things, which then can't be tied up, and so become impossible to finish.

- Output regularly, ideally once a year.
- Don't let projects contain too much.
- Reduce to smaller pieces.

Or create your great masterpiece but make it a compilation of earlier, smaller outputs.

The filled page is seductive, hypnotic. It mesmerises us. However it only becomes complete when it goes outside into the world.

- Even if it's imperfect, let it go.
- Even if you're not ready, let it go.

- Even if it has mistakes, let it go.
- Even if you feel sad, let it go.

Remember what I said at the start of the book about the affliction of perfectionism?

You do the best you can, then you send it beyond yourself into the world.

Some of my favourite works of art have mistakes in them. In fact it's the errors that make them human.

So, knowing when to end a project, is a difficult art. Also completion itself is a complex process. It's easy to keep making, but arduous to come to an end. A finish requires application, stamina, determination.

An ending requires –

- Will power.
- Clarity.
- Overview.
- Dedication.

And 30% more work.

The last 10% of any project will require 30% of your overall effort.

In any life, there is the sense that all works are one work. The material is really endless. There is no beginning, no end. It's just one moment.

But in order not to get caught up in this philosophical entanglement, it's useful to set limits on your practice.

So everything that you make in one week/month/year is the show, regardless of what it contains.

Perfect.

I've also set boundaries at the start of a project. So, for example, I will make a piece every month or every day for a year and exhibit it as ongoing process.

What gets shown is the work.

But the dark circus of creativity has to end somewhere.

- Even if it's not ready, it has to end.
- Even if I don't like the work, it has to end.
- Even if it's not perfect, it has to end.
- Even if I am embarrassed, it has to end.

So even though it's not entirely ready, feels premature and unsteady, for me, this is the moment to...

STOP.

The last 10%
of any project
will require
30% of your
overall effort.

MICHAEL ATAVAR

Michael Atavar is an artist and a creative consultant with a practice that mixes creativity, business, art and psychology.

His output includes over thirty public works, in a variety of forms – performance, installation, digital media, publishing.

www.atavar.com
www.how-to-be-an-artist.com
www.12-rules-of-creativity.com
www.everyone-is-creative.com
www.creativepractice.com
www.210cards.com

ACKNOWLEDGEMENTS

Several people supported this project at key stages of development – Amy, Andrea, Andrew, Anil, Ben, Crispin, Duncan, Emily, Frances, Frank, Gabrielle, Grita, Hannah, Iain, Isabel, Jonathan, Julian, Karin, Laura, Leah, Lori, Manick, Martin, Nick, Nikki, Philippa, Portland, Rami, Richard, Ritchie, Robert, Ruth, Scott, Stella, Valerie.

Thank you to the many artists who appear as clients in the text. Your contribution is invaluable.

Parts of this volume were written during British Council Artist Links residencies in China and Brazil.

This book is dedicated to the memory of Diane Westhorpe.

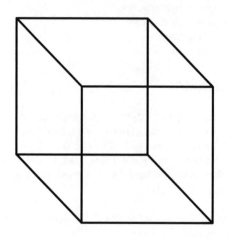